50 WAYS TO SHARE YOUR FAITH

50 Ways
to Share Your Faith

IAN KNOX

GREAT
IDEAS

EASTBOURNE

Unless otherwise indicated, biblical quotations are
from the New International Version © 1973, 1978, 1984
by the International Bible Society.
AV = Authorised version, Crown copyright.

ISBN 0 85476 994 3

Published by
KINGSWAY COMMUNICATIONS LTD
Lottbridge Drove, Eastbourne, BN23 6NT, England.
Email: books@kingsway.co.uk

Book design and production for the publishers by
Bookprint Creative Services, P.O. Box 827, BN21 3YJ, England.
Printed in Great Britain.

Contents

Acknowledgements

This book could not have been written without major help from the many people who, down the years, have encouraged and instructed me in the sharing of my Christian faith with others, both publicly and one-to-one. I am especially grateful to my friends Mike Coe, Penny Frank and Mark Beaumont for allowing me to use some of their expertise, and to draw on lectures given by them to the students of the Birmingham Bible Institute (now the Birmingham Christian College).

Thanks are due, too, to the fantastic team at the 40:3 Trust, the organisation which enables me to be a full-time evangelist. Well done Julie, Sue and Darren for your support, advice and hard work.

But the biggest 'thank you' goes to my wife Ruth, for her constant love and work behind the scenes: it is to her that I dedicate this book.

Why This Book?

'If only . . .'

'If only he were a Christian.'

'If only she knew Jesus.'

'If only I knew how to get through to him.'

'If only I had the right words to say to her.'

Time for a big sigh, a shrug of the shoulders and a feeling of helplessness and hopelessness. Isn't that the way it is?

No, it isn't! It is time for help, and hope, and a lot of know-how. It has been said that something in the order of 97 per cent of all Christians have never led another person to Christ. You have got this book to see if you can get into the 3 per cent. Good news – you can!

Welcome to the wonderful world of faith-sharing, where your most pressing questions will find an answer, and the person with whom you would most like to speak about Jesus will be identified and highlighted as a potential new Christian.

As your guide and mentor I admit to wearing large, invisible 'L' plates. I have failed the test many times. But I know the best personal evangelist ever, and he is the winner. Jesus will be our real guide and mentor. He has been my teacher and inspiration since, without my really realising what I was doing, I helped my sister become a Christian when I was nine years old. With a few friends I started a Christian Union at my secondary school when I was 15, and I have been preaching since I was 17.

I will be drawing on some of the lectures I gave during five years as Director of Evangelism at the Birmingham Bible Institute (now the Birmingham Christian College), and on my book *100 Faith-Sharing Talks* (Kingsway Publications). But mainly I will be drawing on nearly 50 years of sharing my faith with others, both as a preacher (for 40 of those years) and in countless personal encounters. Much of my experience is through terrible errors, gaffes, faux pas and howling mistakes. There seem to have been far fewer 'successes', alas. Perhaps you will learn from my mistakes.

I promise you this: if you are allowed by Jesus to lead one other person to Christ, it will be one of the ultimately great events in your whole life. Don't let the devil get in the way: read all of the sections including 'The Big Questions' and 'The Keys', pick out the people who are special to you highlighted in 'The 50' and then – go for it! Don't be afraid – the Lord your God is with you (Joshua 1:9).

The Big Questions

Why Bother?

There are some Christians who never speak about their faith. 'It's a private thing between me and God.' Others seem to make it their one topic of conversation, whether anyone else wants to hear or not. Most of us are somewhere in between, occasional talkers, often hesitantly or reluctantly. Why do we bother?

Just do it!

Reason number one is a real hot potato these days, when we all like doing our own thing. It is simply because Jesus tells us that this is what he wants us to do. Christianity is about choices, but it is even more about obedience. Who is Jesus? 'You call me "Teacher" and "Lord", and rightly so, for that is what I am,' he told his disciples (John 13:13). This was in the context of his serving them, as he had washed their feet, so he was not being bossy! But he spoke the truth: he is Lord (Philippians 2:11).

At the very beginning of his ministry, he told his first followers they would be 'fishers of men' (Mark 1:17). The problem for us is that our church can be so cosy, full of love and fellowship, that it takes up all of our time and all our friends are there. It was the Texan, C. V. Hill, who pointed out: 'We are to be fishers of men, not keepers of the

15

aquarium.' Jesus sends us out to reach others for his kingdom. 'I have other sheep that are not of this sheep pen. I must bring them also' (John 10:16) is another way he pictures the work in hand.

OK – then let him get on with it. Yes – but – he insists on our joining in. His last words to all his friends were, 'You will be my witnesses' (Acts 1:8). Sadly, for many of us, he made no exceptions. What about that unknown disciple, James (not the brother of John, but the other James)? He never says a word in all four Gospels – perhaps he is the strong (or, even, the weak) silent type. But does he remain quiet? Apparently not.

Or what about Thomas, who always seems to say the wrong thing and is full of doubts – can he escape? Surely he should wait until he is more secure in his faith, more able to be relied on? The end of Matthew's Gospel is a blow to him for it tells us that before the Ascension 'some doubted' (Matthew 28:17), but 'then Jesus came to them' (those doubters) and told them to 'go and make disciples' (verses 18–19). This is not what reluctant doubters want to hear!

It is a problem. We all want to grab hold of the final promise, 'I am with you always to the very end of the age' (verse 20). However, this is given in the context of getting out and sharing our faith. As the old song said about love and marriage going together like a horse and carriage, 'You can't have one without the other'. It is a tough one, but Christianity is ultimately not a democracy: sharing our faith is what Jesus expects us to do, and we are not voting on it.

Help me!

If reason one is to be taken on the chin, reason two for sharing our faith is to be taken in the hand. Look at the world out there – even the little bit of it where you are. Are things going well spiritually? Is there happiness, peace and security, or has it all gone wrong?

Way back in the Old Testament, one of the great prophets is told something serious about himself and the people around him. Grab a Bible and read Ezekiel 33 up to verse 11. It is good, strong, emotive stuff. Here is pictured a world, not only in a mess but in danger. Ezekiel is the man with the answer: he knows God can work a great rescue act. He also realises that, unless this happens, the situation will become intolerable. God's words to him are unequivocal: 'Son of man, I have made you a watchman' (Ezekiel 33:7).

We will look at this in more detail under 'Who Is Out There?'. Enough at the moment to say that there is a world out there that is starving for the bread of life (John 6:35), parched for the water of life (John 7:38), and dying for the kiss of life (John 14:6). With the food, drink and revival in our possession, it is imperative to hand these to those who have no hope otherwise.

I'm ready

I am constantly surprised about one thing in faith-sharing: the fear I experience is my own fault. When I do share my faith I rarely receive any abuse – I cannot remember the last time I did. People seem, at worst, neutral. If I speak in the right way, and at the right time (Key 3 and Key 4, coming in the next section), I am amazed and (to be honest) embarrassed at the joy with which my stumbling words are greeted.

Jesus was right: the fields are ripe for harvest (John 4:35). The 'opposition', more often than not, is not opposing us at all. People are exactly as Jesus pictured them, 'harassed and helpless, like sheep without a shepherd' (Matthew 9:36). The problem is not the harvest but the lack of workers to bring it in (Matthew 9:37). Many would love to receive our good news. In their world so much seems to go wrong. No one has told them that we have discovered the one person with the remedy. Of course, in reality, it was he who discovered us, and gave us a brand new life.

Now there are others, like us, who are waiting for good answers to their ultimate life questions. God pictures them as 'Multitudes, multitudes in the valley of decision' (Joel 3:14). 'Come over . . . and help us,' they cry (Acts 16:9). That is why we share our faith: others want us to.

'The girl can't help it'

These words of an old song title give the best of reasons for sharing our faith. It is because it is so brilliant, I've got to tell someone else, or I'll go crazy bottling it up inside me.

Do you know, I have been forgiven all my sins by a holy God, whose Son Jesus washed me completely clean from all of them (1 John 1:7)? I have a new life, which will last for ever, guaranteed by the one who gave it to me (John 10:28). He has given me the greatest life imaginable, life in all its fullness (John 10:10). My being is at peace with God through Jesus (Romans 5:1), my spirit is bouncing along with a new joy (John 15:11) and my heart is overwhelmed by the love of Jesus (John 15:9). I have been given a sense of direction in my life (John 14:6) and a heavenly destination (John 14:2). Even my mind has grown to include the very mind of this greatest person who ever lived (1 Corinthians 2:16). It is so amazing, even sensational.

Do you never feel like Peter and John, standing in front of the Jewish ruling body, and saying to them, 'We cannot help speaking about what we have seen and heard' (Acts 4:20)? Our faith is too good to keep. We want to give it away. When we do, we find it grows in us, rather than diminishing like a cake where there are only so many slices to hand out. Who wants to be like little Jack Horner, sitting in his corner, keeping his pie all to himself?

Why bother faith-sharing? Maybe some of us do it

because we *want* to do it, and never mind the other three reasons, even though they lack the selfishness of this last reason.

That's settled, then. Now to the next Big Question.

Who Does It?

This faith-sharing – is it all down to me? Don't panic: help is at hand. You are not on your own. There will be some practical suggestions, as you realise your own limitations, in Key 5. For this Big Question there are three answers.

Evangelists

I am biased about this first category, as well as being stuck with it, because I am an evangelist. Perhaps to help those who are evangelists not to get too big-headed, the whole Bible uses the word only three times. One man, Philip, is specifically called an evangelist (Acts 21:8). In Ephesians 4:11 a series of leadership gifts is set out, with 'evangelists' right in the middle. They are there, like other leaders, to help the body of Christ to grow. We will see the third reference in a moment.

The evangelist is given a specific gift from the Holy Spirit to help others into God's Kingdom. He or she stands at the door and says, 'Come in, you're welcome.' It is rather like a midwife helping at the birth of a child. To put it another way, the evangelist has a combine harvester to help the farmer gather in the ripened wheat. The baby is not hers, the harvest is not his, but her or his help is of great value at the appropriate time.

Who has the gift of evangelism in your church and area? Do you use their help from time to time? They are sure to have some good ideas for you personally, as well as being able to speak at meetings and to individual people. God's gifts are for us to use. Don't ignore or sideline someone who is specifically gifted to help others meet Jesus.

Church leaders

The third reference to 'evangelist' in the Bible is in 2 Timothy 4:5, where Paul tells his protégé, the young church leader Timothy, to 'do the work of an evangelist'. It would seem that he does not have the Ephesians 4 gift, but Paul tells him to get on with it anyway. The word 'work' suggests he will not find it easy.

Perhaps we expect too much of our leaders in the church, as if they should be experts in every aspect of the Christian life. They will be the first to admit that this is far from reality. However, they are called by God to help others to meet Christ by doing this 'work of an evangelist'. They should be able to help you in your faith-sharing. For example, has your church ever had a preaching/teaching series on the practical and spiritual aspects of faith-sharing? The church I attend did that for a month not long ago. It was not only hugely appreciated, but packed out for each service. Our minister decided to hold each meeting at a normal Sunday service, both so that the maximum number could benefit, and to show that this was central to our church's life and ministry, not a peripheral 'extra'.

It is worth remembering that Jesus sent out his new leaders to faith-share two by two (Mark 6:7). Even they were not good enough to go it alone. We need to be in there, helping and encouraging our leaders and getting them alongside us.

Every Christian

You didn't think you were going to sneak out of this, did you? We have already looked at the all-inclusive nature of

'You shall be my witnesses' (Acts 1:8). There are two other areas to consider here.

When I was young, our minister would often quote from Matthew 10:32–33: 'Whoever acknowledges me before men, I will also acknowledge him before my Father in heaven. But whoever disowns me before men, I will disown him before my Father in heaven.' It always seemed a bit threatening, a sort of 'do it, or else . . .'. But they are the words of Jesus and need to be taken seriously. The word 'whoever' does not give me an escape clause. What does it mean?

It means that I need to understand fully the classic definition of a Christian given by Paul in Romans 10:9–10:

> If you confess with your mouth, 'Jesus is Lord,' and believe in your heart that God raised him from the dead, you will be saved. For it is with your heart that you believe and are justified, and it is with your mouth that you confess and are saved.

To be a Christian, I need to speak of my faith to others. Paul sees this of such vital importance that he puts the 'confession' of belief before the heart's trust. The two are completely inseparable, rather like a new-born baby proving it is alive by crying out. We have been guilty too often in our Western Christianity of permitting our faith to be strictly personal and private, and we need to get our teaching back on a biblical basis. If I am to be a Christian, I will both believe and confess by word of mouth the reality of my faith. Not to speak of Jesus is to deny the very basis of my relationship with him. In an emergency, we can even use this as our excuse for saying something! Hopefully it will not come to that.

Where Do I Begin?

I practised for some years as a lawyer. The profession is full of its own wonderful jargon, often in Latin. One or two expressions still linger in my memory, among which is *sine qua non*. This is something without which no progress can be made, literally 'without which, not'.

There is *sine qua non* in faith-sharing. It is the easily missed bit in Mark 1:17. Jesus is calling Simon and Andrew to be his first disciples, and he says to them, 'Come, follow me, and I will make you fishers of men.' It is a very clever invitation, for he speaks in the specific language of their current occupation of fishermen. Ever since then, Christians have drawn on these words as their inspiration to go out to 'fish' for others. The beginning of the invitation has also been a guide as to what it means to become a Christian – to hear and obey the call of Jesus, 'Come, follow me.'

There is, with these two great parts to the verse, a real danger of missing the vital *sine qua non* in the middle. If we are to go with Jesus and reach out to others, we can only do it effectively if we receive the strength of the words 'I will make you'. From first to last in faith-sharing, Jesus must be the one who makes it happen. The disciples, with all their personal contact with Jesus over three years, and their face-to-face meetings with the risen Christ, were still told to 'stay

. . . until you have been clothed with power from on high'
(Luke 24:49).

To work under our own power is a recipe for failure. Jesus
quoted from Isaiah 61 about his own faith-sharing:

> 'The Spirit of the Lord is on me,
> because he has anointed me
> to preach good news to the poor.
> He has sent me to proclaim freedom
>   for the prisoners
> and recovery of sight for the blind,
> to release the oppressed,
> to proclaim the year of the Lord's favour.'
>
> (Luke 4:18–19)

How did Jesus fulfil his ministry and share the 'good
news'? Answer: 'the Spirit of the Lord' was on him. If he
needed that help, the corollary is obvious: how much more
do we? That is where to start: 'Lord, fill me with your Holy
Spirit, right now.' Nor is this a one-off, at least not for me. I
go with Billy Graham here. He was asked why he said he
needed to be filled over and over again with the Holy Spirit.
His answer is a classic: 'Because I leak.' 'Be filled with the
Spirit' (Ephesians 5:18) is a verb in the present continuous
imperative (the joys of language!): 'Go on all the time being
filled' is a better way of putting it.

And if Jesus needed to get up and pray (Mark 1:35),
some serious praying will give us the confidence to go in
God's strength to share our faith. This is where to begin, in
our personal relationship with our heavenly Father, made
'fishers' by Jesus, filled with his Holy Spirit. Our words will
then be an outpouring of the life of faith already deep in
our beings.

We will look further at having the right sort of life in
Key 3. For the moment, there are two simple answers to

'Where do I begin?' One: let Jesus, by his Spirit, fill your life and make you into a 'fisher'. Two: have a life of trusting prayer. Simple? Yes – it can happen in a moment, but it also takes a lifetime of practice. It's high time to get started.

Who Is Out There?

What are these people like – these people with whom I should be sharing my faith? While generalisations may be somewhat glib, I can assure you that 'these people' are not Martians, nor do they have two heads. They are quite normal!

Jesus did a lovely thing for Paul when he sent him to share his faith. He described the condition of Paul's potential audience so he would know what he was facing. Paul tells us exactly what Jesus said, during his testimony before King Agrippa in Acts 26. After his amazing conversion on the Damascus road, Jesus told him that he was being sent to the non-Jewish world and then described the people in that world and their needs.

I believe that the five things Paul discovered that day are for us in the twenty-first century, and that those with whom we share our faith have the same needs and potential. These are the words of Jesus to Paul (Acts 26:17–18):

> 'I am sending you to them to open their eyes and turn them from darkness to light, and from the power of Satan to God, so that they may receive forgiveness of sins and a place among those who are sanctified through faith in me.'

So – what are 'these people' like? One or more of the following will be true.

People are blind

Paul was sent by Jesus 'to open their eyes'. So are we. Often today the 'blindness' is one of sheer ignorance. In 1955, 80 per cent of people in the United Kingdom said they had been to Sunday school as children. Most people therefore knew something about God, Jesus and the Bible. By 1997, among all young people, 87 per cent said that they had no contact with God at all, whether it was through family, school, church or friends. Colleagues of mine who visit secondary schools have posed the question, 'What is a Christian?' Answers have included, 'Someone who believes in reincarnation,' and 'A person who grows his own vegetables.'

I also find a great 'blindness' when it comes to a sense of assurance in knowing Jesus personally. This is true even among good churchgoers, especially older ones. I had been speaking about God's salvation at an Anglican church one Sunday. Afterwards an older man approached me. 'I've been in this church choir for 51 years,' he said. 'I've been the church-warden for ten years. But as for being saved – I just don't know.' Others have simply not 'seen' it. Another man told me, after trusting Christ, 'You've put a light in my life that I didn't know existed.' Even though it was really Jesus who did it, I knew what he meant.

As Jesus said that part of his own mission was to bring the 'recovery of sight for the blind' (Luke 4:18), so we are 'to open their eyes'. You must have heard of the lady who went into a jeweller's wanting a gold cross for a necklace. The shop assistant produced a tray of crosses. 'Oh look,' she said, as she picked one up. 'There's a little man on one of these. I wonder what he's doing there!' This true story is a health warning to all of us faith-sharers. Blind spiritual eyes need to be opened to the loveliness of Jesus, the glory of God and the splendour of his salvation.

People are in darkness

I believe we are living in a society where more and more people have real, deep needs which can only be met by Jesus. This is so even among those who are rich, famous and clever. A friend of mine told me recently, after successfully climbing to the top of his profession, 'I've just retired after working there for over 20 years. I have no idea why I did the job.' Many realise that they have climbed the ladder of success, only to find that they put their ladder against the wrong wall in the first place.

Why has work become a 'darkness' for so many? Who can give a real meaning to life? We have met the one who says, 'I am the way' (John 14:6). The church I attend has a big university within its area. More than one leading professor in scientific subjects has said to our leaders: 'Please don't just teach us intellectually in church. Give us something for our hearts – that's why we come.' The one-time richest man in the world, the late John D. Rockerfeller, was asked, 'How many millions does it take to make you happy?' His reply was salutary: 'The next one.'

If success and riches leave their possessors in 'darkness', many more have particularly obvious 'darknesses'. We will look specifically in 'The 50' at helping those who are in the darkness of bereavement. One marriage in two now ends in divorce: a real darkness for those involved, not least the children. 'All the lonely people' about whom the Beatles sang comprise vast numbers, not only those who live alone but lonely members of families who feel isolated or trapped when surrounded by others.

Who cares for those in the many darknesses of failure, loss, loneliness, purposelessness, pain and suffering? Jesus cares. He said, 'I am the light of the world. Whoever follows me will never walk in darkness, but will have the light of life' (John 8:12).

People are under the power of Satan

Sin is not an 'in' word. Sin is equated with the wild excesses described in the more sensational sections of the media – murders, rapes, drug-smuggling and so on. But we have been shown in our own lives that anyone who does any wrong becomes sin's 'slave' (John 8:34). Sin has spoiled us all individually and the world collectively. Sin is at the root of all our problems because we are below God's perfect glory (Romans 3:23). At the same time, Christians know that God's Son, Jesus, is the one who can make us completely free (John 8:36), cleaning us up from all sin (1 John 1:7).

Antoine de Saint-Exupéry, in his brilliant book *Wind, Sand and Stars*, says, 'We all yearn to escape from prison.' As we look at people who need to know Jesus, we realise how wonderful it would be if Satan's grip on their lives could be prised away, and that the new embrace of Jesus would be such a blessing.

People can be forgiven

This is the positive way of looking at the negative of Satan's hold. Jesus has died and been raised from the dead to enable us to 'receive forgiveness of sins'. The very first command of Jesus in his first-ever sermon was 'Repent' (Mark 1:15). People need to turn through 180 degrees from their sin to see the Lord Jesus, and to receive his total for ever forgiveness.

For some, this may come after the light shines into their darkness. For others it is a first step. For everyone it is vital at some stage. John Stott, in *Christian Mission in the Modern World*, asserts, 'Forgiveness remains man's chief need and an indispensable part of the good news.' My experience is that most people know they need to be forgiven by God. Indeed, the problem is sometimes that people feel they have got their lives too wrong. A very distinguished lady once said to me,

'I'm too bad to be a Christian.' I was able to reassure her with the great words in Luke 15:2, where the very enemies of Jesus said of him, 'This man welcomes sinners.'

People can become God's people

Jesus taught that we have a place among those who are sanctified by faith in him. I am in the eternal family of God. It is really true when I pray to 'Our Father'. I have a new life, with sight, light, freedom from Satan and complete forgiveness.

Christianity is partly about deliverance from the negatives, but it is much more about a new and eternal relationship with the Living God. It is not just about what people are like, but about what – and who – they can become in Christ. As you wonder what people are like, view them also as they will be when they come to Jesus Christ and he comes to them. That's the way to see them – with him!

How Will People React?

Here is a trivia quiz question: who was Aldo Guiffré? Clue: the movies. Second clue: he was Il Brutto. Oh come on. A further clue: Lee van Cleef was Il Malo. Yet more help: Clint Eastwood was Il Buono.

Answer: Aldo was the Ugly in *The Good, the Bad and the Ugly*, which some would say was the best of all the 'spaghetti' westerns.

Our final Big Question seeks to find an answer to how people will react to our faith-sharing, and I will draw on our three movie anti-heroes to give the main attitudes. If you want to read of all three, Acts 14:1–21 is an excellent real-life example, and I will refer to it. Paul and Barnabas are sharing the good news of Jesus in an area which has since become modern Turkey. The response of the people may be more extreme than we will encounter, but it is a helpful guide.

The Good: Il Buono

Our two real-life heroes had some good days. 'They spoke so effectively that a great number of Jews believed' (verse 2). It took a while, as they 'spent a considerable time there' (verse 3). God was clearly at work, including 'miraculous signs and wonders' (verse 3). The recipe for success is all here: careful speaking, time given and God making all the difference. No wonder 'a great number' responded positively by believing.

We should be on the look-out for 'the good', who want to say 'Yes' to Jesus. When Jesus sent out his disciples to faith-share, they were told to search out a 'man of peace' who would welcome them (Luke 10:5–7). Sometimes I find myself speaking at a meeting where the atmosphere is none too helpful. I always remind myself that there will be those who are being warmed by God's love and will react positively.

In these days I find more and more people seem glad to hear the good news. Fewer than ever appear worse than neutral. If you expect a good reaction, you may well get one. It will certainly prevent your speaking in a negative or defensive way, which would be counterproductive in any event.

I have started with the good response, because I find it from the majority. But – be prepared!

The Bad: Il Malo

'The people were divided' (verse 4). They still are. A choice has to be made in the end to be for Jesus – or not. Paul and Barnabas found that there were those 'who refused to believe' (verse 2).

We will always feel saddened by those who say 'No' to Jesus. It may be because of a deliberate decision, or because the devil, bad as he is, prevents a response at a particular moment. Paul was later to write, 'The god of this age has blinded the minds of unbelievers, so that they cannot see the light of the gospel of the glory of Christ, who is the image of God' (2 Corinthians 4:4). It is natural to back away from God: only through the kiss of life from Jesus can we come alive (Ephesians 2:1). Archbishop George Carey has said, 'People instinctively run away from the living God.'

In this spiritual battle for the souls of human beings, 'Il

Malo', the bad one, is wandering round, looking to devour people as a lion would. We must resist him (1 Peter 5:8–9). If people do say 'No', that is their absolute right, and we do not read of Paul and Barnabas raving and screaming against such. Even when someone knows the truth, they may turn from it.

The Ugly: Il Brutto

What fortunate people we are who live in the tolerant Western world! The ugly rarely, if ever, rears its head. For Paul and Barnabas 'there was a plot . . . to ill-treat them and stone them' (Acts 14:5). In the end they succeeded: 'They stoned Paul' (verse 19). Brave man that he was, he moved on to the next town (verse 20) and 'they preached the good news in that city' where, once again, they 'won a large number of disciples' (verse 21).

In many parts of the world faith-sharing is a dangerous occupation. Every day Christians die for their beliefs. We in the West are most unlikely to meet strong opposition, and any violence would result in a criminal prosecution. Il Brutto does not stalk us, so of whom are we afraid? But he is a reminder that 'our struggle is not against flesh and blood, but against the rulers, against the authorities, against the powers of this dark world and against the spiritual forces of evil in the heavenly realms' (Ephesians 6:12). If our fellow Christians in countries of oppression are so bold in sharing their faith, why do we not get on with it? I heard Bishop Simon Barrington-Ward say, 'It must cost you no less than everything to follow Jesus.'

Whatever the reaction, Paul and Barnabas went looking for others who would hear and receive their good news. Like them, let us get on with it!

The Keys

Key 1: Know Your Subject

French has never been one of my strengths. I scraped through at 'O' level, and gained another 'O' level pass at 'A' level: the award for those who failed to get an 'A' level pass! However, I was marginally better at it than my wife (or so she claimed), which left me with the sorry task of helping each of our children with the wretched subject as they approached their GCSE French exams. It was back to basics, and a continuous desperate attempt to keep one page ahead. More by their own efforts than through my feeble guidance they all passed. It was not really my subject, but I worked on it for love of our children.

Are you getting my drift? Most Christians feel that faith-sharing is beyond them because they have no idea what to say. If we are really honest what we mean is: 'I don't know my subject, so how can I know what I'm talking about?' This simple admission is the first step forward. Ignorance is curable! It is not a disease for which there is no remedy: knowledge is around the corner. It will mean hard work, but our aim should be the same as that given by Paul to his protégé Timothy: 'Do your best to present yourself to God as one approved, a workman who does not need to be ashamed and who correctly handles the word of truth' (2 Timothy 2:15).

As I had to get into books about French for my children,

so each one of us needs to get into the ultimate guide to faith-sharing, the Bible. If we want to know what to say and how to say it, the Bible has the answers. What is your response to this question: How many Bible verses do I know which would enable me to share my faith? Count them. I asked a whole church that, and only four people could get beyond ten. It does matter, because God's word is the basis for why we believe what we believe. Your own story is important, and we shall look at this in detail in Key 3, but a knowledge of the Bible is indispensable.

Where do you begin? Why not start with a verse that is precious to you? Was there a sentence or two that helped you when you came to trust Christ? Many people have become Christians with the words of Jesus in Revelation 3:20: 'Here I am! I stand at the door and knock. If anyone hears my voice and opens the door, I will come in.' It explains, very simply, the love of Jesus in coming to our very heart's door, waiting for our invitation to enter and change our lives. Why not learn it by heart right now?

The other primary verse is John 3:16: 'God so loved the world that he gave his one and only Son, that whoever believes in him shall not perish but have eternal life.' You may not need much more than that, because it touches on so much: our problem (perishing), God's love, the life and death of Jesus, his risen and eternal life, and our need to respond by believing in him (not in a set of rules). The whole meeting between Jesus and Nicodemus (John 3:1–21) is a great example of one-to-one faith-sharing. It demonstrates how to cut through spurious arguments and shows the need for a radical life-change. The personal encounters in the following two chapters make excellent case studies, too.

As you progress, consider the following verses. Remember, this book is not only for reading, but for using: keep stopping and learning as you go through it. Check out Romans

3:23 for the perfect definition of our wrong-doing: it compares us with God, not with each other. Romans 6:23 shows the two sides of the story, and God's generosity. Go on, look them up – and learn them! The welcome of Jesus is in John 6:37. The change is in John 1:12. The new relationship with God is found in Romans 5:1. The giving of the Holy Spirit is in Luke 11:13.

I want to remove the panic factor from your life, so here are a couple of suggestions. You will get all you need if you read through the Gospel of John and Paul's letter to the Romans. Have a notebook and scribble down the verses which jump out and say 'Use me!'.

A case study

A second suggestion: turn with me now to John 10:1–30. You may not need to go anywhere else, and it will save you flicking from page to page if you are showing it to an interested friend. Let's look at these verses, with bullet points.

- The problem: verse 10. We are being destroyed by evil. Verse 16: we are away from God.
- The danger: verse 1. We try to get in by our own efforts: 'I did it my way'.
- The love of Jesus: verse 11. He dies for us.
- The proof: verses 17 and 18. Jesus dies – and rises again.
- The way in: verse 9. Jesus is 'the gate'.
- The invitation: verse 9. Come on in!
- The new life: verse 10. 'Life . . . to the full.'
- The cost: verse 3. We are called by Jesus to follow him, and are known as belonging to him.
- The personal relationship: verse 27.
- The guarantee: verses 28 to 30. We are kept eternally safe by Jesus and his Father.

I am sure you can find much more in these verses, but that is a start. It's not too hard, is it? Here is a suggestion. Find someone – anyone who is very friendly – and ask them if you can 'experiment' by walking them through these verses as a practice. Ask God to surprise you with their response!

The 'one day' encouragement

In case you are feeling that a large amount of work is needed before you can open your mouth, here is a final boost at the end of Key 1. Flip back from John 10 to John 1:43–47.

Here is a man called Philip. He has responded to the invitation of Jesus to 'Follow me' (verse 43). He has a best friend called Nathaniel, and he wants this friend to meet Jesus. It seems Philip has known Jesus for 24 hours, and is full of the good news that Jesus is the one they have been looking for (verse 44). He is met with a very tricky theological question (verse 45) which would have sunk most people. What can he do?

Philip has no clever answers, but with a simple three-word invitation, 'Come and see' (verse 46), he brings his friend Nathaniel to Jesus, and Jesus turns Nathaniel into one of the founder-disciples of Christianity. Isn't that encouraging? We will never have all the answers. But we know a man who does. Don't use this as an excuse to stay ignorant, but if you have only known Jesus for as little as a day, you can still help someone else to meet him (see Key 7).

Key 2: Know Your Person

Do you want to know something revolutionary? People are not 'souls to be saved'. No! People are people whom Jesus wants to make complete. Jesus said, 'I have come that they may have life, and have it to the full' (John 10:10).

If we want to help someone become a Christian, Jesus Christ is enormously interested in that person as a complete person. If he feels that way, so should we. This means a willingness on our part to share our lives with them and let them share their lives with us. Here are a few pointers.

Who?

Our churches have become such cosy clubs that almost all our friends are there, card-carrying members of the same holy club. Many Christians openly admit that they know fewer and fewer people with whom they need to share their faith. We know our neighbours as nodding acquaintances at best. We are not members of any secular organisations. At work, we are too busy to form relationships. Our modes of transport are isolationist.

This cannot be right, and it is not difficult to rectify. It will mean reprioritising our time, which could include (shock, horror) dropping one or two overtly 'church' activities. 'Neighbour' implies being 'neighbourly', whether it be where we live or where we work. A couple of minutes passing the time of day will lead to an acquaintanceship turning into a friendship. Without pushing or manipulating the situation, a positive approach is the way.

Let me give a simple example. We moved to a house next door to an older couple. Soon after we arrived, there was a great storm. A branch blew down from our neighbours' tree and fell across their driveway. I went round with my saw and offered to cut the branch off for the lady and pull it out of the way, so her husband would not drive into it. It was no great deal, but it led to an immediate friendship. Particularly since he became a widower we have had the strongest links, which have enabled many deeply spiritual conversations to happen quite naturally. We have talked about Jesus, and prayed together, and it all started with a simple neighbourly act.

Here is another one. We live in a typical suburban environment, where we all nod to each other, smile, and live our own lives. How can the ice be broken? Easily. Hold a 'New Year's Day Breakfast'. Mega-amounts of breakfast cereal, eggs, bacon, sausages, toast, marmalade (you get the idea) are stocked up. A silly invitation is circulated both to church members and to every neighbour in the vicinity – no exceptions. 'Who wants to cook breakfast after a New Year's Eve night out? Come round to our place, and we'll do it for you! Any time between 10 a.m. and 3 p.m.' Provide details of who you are and the address, and away you go. The amazing thing is the non-Christian neighbours will drop you a line to say they will be there, bring a small present and write a note of appreciation. None of your Christian church friends will do any of these, though they will turn up! However, the interaction between both groups will be excellent, and you will have loads of neighbours you now know. (A bonus is that no one expects alcohol with their breakfast, so you don't need to serve it!)

Where?

What are you interested in – apart from church? What are you doing about it? Are you sharing your life within those interests, and with others who share those concerns? Here are some hot words from Paul, in 1 Corinthians 9:19–23:

> Though I am free and belong to no man, I make myself a slave to everyone, to win as many as possible. . . . I have become all things to all men so that by all possible means I might save some. I do all this for the sake of the gospel, that I may share in its blessings.

What is he talking about? We use the expression 'all things to all men' nowadays to suggest compromise, but Paul is saying the opposite. He is getting alongside people where they are in order to win them for Christ. He loves them enough to share their interests. As we identify with our world around us, so that world will move nearer to us and be willing to hear what we have to say. If we stay away until we want to 'convert' them, they will see through us and despise our obvious attempts at proselytisation.

When I was at university, the Christian Union was famous for its non-participation in the affairs of the Student Union. Once a year the Debating Society put on a religious debate, and it was a matter of open derision that the Christian Union would turn up for this but for no other debate. They seemed to have no interest in student concerns of a local, national or international nature. No wonder Christianity made little or no impact on the university. Many overtly Christian battles have been lost in the nation in recent years:

could it be because we Christians are not committed to other causes and our voice is therefore not heard when it matters to us?

Get into a secular club or organisation. Play or watch sport. Get to know people. Dare to go clubbing and pubbing, and have the strength to be a real Christian in those places. What would Jesus have done?

When?

Time is vital. But have we time for people, especially at their points of need? Will we pop round when they need a friend? Could we baby-sit? Does someone need a lift to the hospital to see a relative? Have we time to visit a neighbour or work colleague in that hospital?

Opportunities arise naturally when help is wanted. Seize the day. A work colleague of mine, who was a very intimidating person, had to have a major operation. I sent a card saying I was praying for God's healing. When my colleague returned, I was given a big hug and assured that I had said the one thing they had wanted to read at that time. I had written with some trepidation, but it turned our relationship around. I have found really 'tough' neighbours who have not only valued a hospital visit but have held my hand ('hard' men) and cried as I have prayed with them.

I realise that all this sounds as if I am a genius at this, whereas I am a raw beginner. I am for ever learning that a major key to faith-sharing is earning the right to do so. I need to make and maintain friendships. I must be at least as interested in others, and what they say and think, as I want them to be in what I have to share.

When I do this, I discover that faith-sharing becomes easy. As long as the other Keys are in place, this Key enables me to custom-fit the good news to the individual. I do not need a set formula, as each person is unique, as we shall see further in Keys 6 and 7. A friend of mine put it like this: 'Stay close to God. Stay close to people. Bring God and people together.'

Key 3: Know Your Saviour

Hang on, don't miss this one out! It's not the same as Key 1. There have been some people who know all there is to know under Key 1 who have lost (or never had) this.

If you are going to be of real value in faith-sharing, you need to be very close to Jesus. All salvation comes from him, not us. We need to know his love, his way and his plan. We can never say, 'Go to Jesus.' It must always be 'Come to Jesus.' The closer we are to his heart, the more we will love those with whom we are sharing, and the more we will get Keys 4 and 7 right.

That is why the Holy Spirit and prayer are crucial. A good word must come from a good life. People will consider what they see before they believe what they hear. I have found it helpful to study my Bible, not only for knowledge of my faith to share but also for a life of faith to live. It is good to know; it is better to be. I have been greatly helped in my personal Christian life by the fellowship of others and the advice of a personal pastor. Do you have anyone who keeps an eye on your spiritual life?

A story to tell

If you are enjoying a present experience of knowing Jesus, you will have something constant and up-to-date to share.

46

Do not hide behind false modesty, because you do have a story to tell. It will be the story of how Jesus not only met and changed you, but of what he means to you today and is currently doing with you and for you.

It might help your sharing if you work out a few pointers. You might even like to write them down for your eyes only. Here are a few hints (I'm grateful to my friend and fellow-evangelist Mike Coe for his thoughts on this).

- What was your background before you and Jesus got together? Don't pull your family down if you can help it.
- Why were you *not* a Christian?
- What changed your mind?
- How did you become a Christian?
- What difference has Jesus made – then and now?
- What has been going on in the last year; the last month; this week?
- There is no need to kid on that you are perfect: owning up to 'L' plates and mistakes will help rather than hinder.
- Keep It Simple, Stupid (K.I.S.S.)! Big Bible words and spiritual jargon will be wasted. Work out how to speak in a way people can understand.
- Listen to questions, so your story is relevant to your contact.
- Tell the truth, speaking of the hard times as well as the good. Don't exaggerate.
- Speak positively, showing how good Jesus is, as are his gifts.
- It's a bad idea to discredit others, including your church.
- Be enthusiastic, and be the person God is making you, not aping another Christian's testimony.

That is plenty of do's and don'ts! Here is the best advice:

> In your hearts set apart Christ as Lord. Always be prepared to give an answer to everyone who asks you to give the reason for the hope that you have. (1 Peter 3:15)

Key 4: Know Your Time

Key 3 comes first: only then can you hit this one. When should we share our faith with someone else? We should be doing this, whether we like it or not, every moment by the way we live. But the answer on verbal communication is in Ecclesiastes 3:1 and 7:

> There is a time for everything,
> and a season for every activity under heaven:
> . . . a time to be silent and a time to speak.

If ever we needed the help of the Holy Spirit, it is at this point. At one time it is right to speak up. On another occasion it is better to shut up. Only the nudge of the Holy Spirit will enable us to get it right. That inner conviction is crucial.

With one person it is best to get right in and tell them of your faith there and then. With another (as Key 5 will show) you may rarely, if ever, have the chance to speak of spiritual things. In another situation, it may be 'not now – wait'. Let me explain.

Many years ago I used to be the 'padre' (the one who gave the Christian talks) at an all-male youth camp. The very first year went well, and a number of guys became Christians. I told them to tell their parents as soon as they got home. The incomparable Herbert Hackett was in charge of the camp.

He wisely told me that my advice would have been better with a word of caution built in to the effect that God would guide each person as to the correct moment to speak. His counsel was right, and I would now suggest a compromise.

A teenage young man becomes a Christian at a Sunday evening church service (or at the youth group afterwards). How and when should he share his faith with his non-committal parents? Should he walk in behind a big black Bible and tell them they are both sinners on their way to hell? Or (I bet you are hoping for an alternative) is there a better way? What about a simple smile and a 'Goodnight'? Then the next day, make the bed and go to school/college? When Mum looks into the bedroom, she faints across the never-before-made bed. Coming round, she notices the Bible on the bedside table. That afternoon, when our hero comes home, he will be given a curious smile, a cup of tea, and a request to explain if he is feeling well, bearing in mind the tidiness upstairs. That might be a better moment, and a better way. You get the idea?

Opportunities will come from God, and his timing is always perfect. Trust him, and wait for the Holy Spirit's 'now'. But, be careful: it will come. Are you listening? Are you ready?

Key 5: Know Your Limitations

What a relief to reach this key! If you are struggling with everything else, this is your chapter. On the other hand, if you already know everything else, try this one for size.

You may not be the person who helps another particular person become a Christian. Indeed, you may not be the person who faith-shares with them at all. Anything you said could even be counterproductive. You might have to back right off. I hear many a cautionary tale as I preach in various situations, with conversations which go like this:

'Can I have a word with you?' (It is a lady who has approached me at the end of a morning service.)

'Sure.'

'If only my husband had heard that sermon. It was spot-on for him.'

'He's not here?'

'Here! You must be joking. He's at home in bed.'

Thinks . . . lucky bloke. Says: 'Not involved here, then?'

'Wouldn't come near the place.'

'Do you ever talk with him about God?'

'Are you kidding? I'm for ever telling him what a different man he'd be if he was a Spirit-filled born-again Christian.'

Thinks . . . ouch. Says: 'Can I make a suggestion? It's just an idea . . .'

'Please do.'

'Why don't you go home, take him in your arms and say, "Darling, I'm so, so sorry. I've been shoving God down your throat. Forgive me. I promise I'll never talk about God again until you say I can."'

'What?!'

'You're too close to the action. Keeping quiet will give your man a chance to put his defences down. Of course you're still allowed to pray. And you need to ask the men of the church what plans they have to help wives like you who have non-Christian husbands.'

'Will that work?'

'It can't put him off more than he is now. But remember – Jesus loves your husband even more than you do, because you've never died for him. He'll reach him – trust him.'

Whether she will take my cruel-but-kind advice is another matter!

If you are not the right person, what can be done? If you have given it your best shot, and nothing has happened, what is the solution? Here are a few ideas.

Pray

Don't skip this, or take it for granted. God loves to hear our requests. If someone is a burden, give them to him. 'Cast all your anxiety on him because he cares for you' (1 Peter 5:7).

They say 'prayer changes things'. My experience is more that prayer changes people. The person it most seems to change is me and my attitudes. It gives me a love for those I cannot reach to enable me to trust God with them. As I release them to him, he helps me realise that it was his problem all the time. I have a very private 'hit list' I pray for daily, some of whom I may never get to faith-share with personally. I trust them to God.

Give a book

Recently I finished reading an excellent book of daily Bible readings. I got a few copies of it and gave them as Christmas presents to some of the special people I am seeking to share my faith with. One in particular has told me how he is enjoying 'dipping into it'. The book can say all sorts of things at times when he is ready to hear them.

Of course, Key 2 is crucial: you need to match the book to the person and be sure they will not feel 'got at'. It could be an idea to ask them if they would like the book in the first place.

Find a meeting

If someone is showing real interest in Christian things, but you seem to have reached your limit in sharing your faith, why not use the wider church to help? Again, you will need Key 2. What sort of meeting would help further a quest for personal faith? Is the person ready for, and able to cope with, your church? Remember that the services at which you feel at home may seem like a visit to the dark side of the moon for an outsider. At least do a little explaining of what might happen before you go. An informal pub evening put on by the outreach group, with a helpful evangelistic speaker, may work better. What about a gospel concert, if the music is the sort your friend likes?

Realistically, a meeting of any sort may be some way down the spiritual journey. It is a good option at some point.

Phone a friend

Why go it alone? There may well be someone who can help you in your faith-sharing, either with you or for you. Who could that be? I asked nearly 200 people who they would ask to help them.

As you can see from Chart 1 below, the majority chose – not unexpectedly – their partner or a friend. I then asked a second question: 'With whom would you get that person to help you share your faith?' Charts 2 and 3 show the response.

In some cases, the faith-sharing can be done together. A neighbour can be asked round for a coffee and a chat, as the two of you help that neighbour to meet Jesus. In other cases, your partner, or friend, or other 'helper' will be faith-sharing on your behalf. To go back to the conversation at the beginning of this key, a wife will need one or more of the men in the church to play their part. They will need to build their own friendship with her husband, earning the right to talk about spiritual things. They may be able to take him to a men's breakfast or some such similar event where the good news of Jesus will be presented. The wife's only involvement will be in praying.

If the church is to be a body, each member can play their part, not only in faith-sharing but in supporting others who have reached an impasse.

When we have reached the limit of what we can do, God has more resources beyond us. Let's use them.

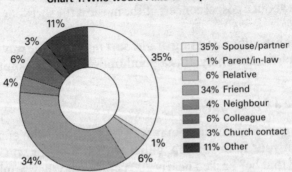

Chart 1: Who would I like to help me?

- 35% Spouse/partner
- 1% Parent/in-law
- 6% Relative
- 34% Friend
- 4% Neighbour
- 6% Colleague
- 3% Church contact
- 11% Other

Chart 2: With the help of my spouse/partner, who would I like to share my faith with?

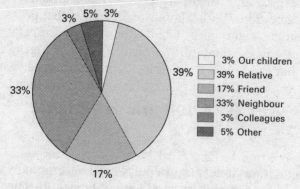

- 3% Our children
- 39% Relative
- 17% Friend
- 33% Neighbour
- 3% Colleagues
- 5% Other

Chart 3: With the help of my friend, who would I like to share my faith with?

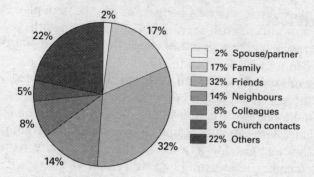

- 2% Spouse/partner
- 17% Family
- 32% Friends
- 14% Neighbours
- 8% Colleagues
- 5% Church contacts
- 22% Others

Key 6: Know the Ambience

I thought it was time we had a fancy heading, especially after my comments about how good I am at French! It is my way of saying that your faith-sharing should have a comfort factor. Let me explain.

Where to be

Here are a few very practical suggestions for faith-sharing:

- Be relaxed. Your nervousness will be communicated, and tension will not help a conversation.
- Find a relaxed situation where you can talk. If you are at home, sit in easy chairs, and enjoy a cup of something and a biscuit. Go for a walk in the park. Share a meal. Remember Jesus sitting by a well (John 4).
- Try to avoid interruptions. Disengage the phone. Ask others not to come into the room.
- If you are in a public place (church, café, pub), it could help if your friend is not sitting where they may be embarrassed by others looking at their face, especially if they were to cry.
- If in private, be very careful about one-to-one intimate chats with the opposite sex.
- Have a little New Testament at the ready but tucked

away: better than a huge, rather threatening, big black Bible.

- Learn to read upside-down, so your friend can read the verse the right way up!
- Make the whole thing natural and normal.

Where to start

The simple and obvious answer as to where to start must be: where the person is. How easy it is to forget this. We have a 'package deal' in our mind (such as Key 7 will suggest). The problem is, your friend may not be at your starting point. I commend a read-through of Philip's meeting with the Ethiopian in Acts 8:26–39. The man has a particular problem, that of understanding a reading from Isaiah. Verse 35 says this: 'Then Philip began with that very passage of Scripture and told him the good news about Jesus.' What excellent faith-sharing. He did not start with, 'You are a sinner.' He began with the man's own questioning. As a result, the man became a Christian.

We need to find the person's need. Are they looking for real meaning in life? Is there a spiritual hang-up? Is there a hurting inside as a result of loneliness, loss, bereavement, redundancy, marriage breakdown or something along those lines? Is it Jesus who is attracting them? Do some gentle probing. It may be your own life and faith which intrigues them: if so, go back to Key 3 for telling your story.

Keep checking on whether you are making yourself understood. Our language can, too easily, become the 'language of Zion', with words having one meaning for us and a quite different connotation (or none at all) to our hearer. 'Grace' may mean 'God's undeserved love' to us. To another it may be what we say before we eat (we say Grace), or the girl down the road (the beautiful Grace), or the Archbishop (His Grace). When Jesus spoke, 'the large crowd listened to him with delight' (Mark 12:37). Ordinary people felt Jesus communicated with them. Once again, K.I.S.S. (Keep It Simple, Stupid!).

Most of all, remember the goal of your faith-sharing, because then you will start towards that goal. Which is? To introduce your friend to Jesus. Everything else is secondary. Lead. Don't point. Don't pull. Don't force. If you lift up Jesus, he will do the rest. Although he was speaking about his cross, these words apply here: 'I, when I am lifted up from the earth, will draw all men to myself' (John 12:32). Go at his pace, and theirs. Then you will come, at the right time (Key 4), to lead them to meet Jesus: on to Key 7.

Key 7: Becoming a Christian

If I could have one wish for you it would be this: that you have the joy of leading another person to Christ. Here are the simple steps.

First, check the end of Key 6. Do you sense the nudge of the Holy Spirit that your friend is ready to let Jesus change their life? As well as waiting for the right time, there can be the other problem of waiting too long.

Every person who comes to Christ does three things, though they may not be aware of them all at the time. These are only a rule of thumb, and are not to be followed too religiously (pardon the unfortunate expression!). For my own benefit, so I do not panic that I might have missed something out, I have cut them down to an A, B and C.

Admit

We come to Jesus Christ because we need to. Our need may be for fulfilment, or for healing, or help, or rescue, but ultimately our need is for forgiveness. The key verse is Romans 3:23, 'All have sinned and fall short of the glory of God.' Happily, it also begins with an 'A'.

For most people, this will be the time to own up to what has gone wrong. Our sin is not how we have fared compared with those whose lives feature in the tabloids, but how we have not lived as splendidly as God intended. It would help if we could be honest here and admit how we ourselves needed (and need) to be forgiven. It is a simple admission. There may be regret, remorse and sorrow, but the word Jesus uses is 'repent' (Mark 1:15). This is a deliberate turning from sin towards him.

This need for forgiveness may not be the only problem. I would not major on it if, for example, I were helping a recently bereaved person, whose need is much more for the love and embrace of Christ.

Believe

As we turn from our sin, we believe that Jesus has the answer by his death on the cross. As we look for new life, we believe he has risen from the dead and can give us eternal life through his Holy Spirit. He can come to us and, by living in our lives, make us new people. The key verse is John 1:29, 'Look, the Lamb of God, who takes away the sin of the world!' (words of John the Baptist). In an older version it says 'Behold, the Lamb of God', which has the advantage of also beginning with the letter 'B'.

I believe that no one becomes a real Christian without believing in Jesus, his death and resurrection. These are central to our faith. I would want to be sure that my friend understood this.

Commit

There must then be a deliberate act of faith, as we give ourselves to Jesus and let him come to live in our hearts and lives. This must include some realisation of the consequences. Jesus will be Lord of all we are and have. Do not back off from explaining the cost of this commitment, as well as the joys and privileges. The key verse is Matthew 11:28, as Jesus says, 'Come to me' (happily, with a 'C').

This is the response to Admit and Believe. It is the specific step of response as we receive God's forgiveness and power. This is the moment when a new life begins.

A prayer of response

Ask your friend if they are ready to take these steps. If they are sure, encourage them to pray out loud, however fearful they may be. If (as is likely) they say they do not know what to pray, simply ask them what they would like to say to God. Help them along, and suggest they turn what they want to say into a prayer.

Don't make it too hard! I would have an outline prayer in my mind, which someone could say with me, along these lines:

> Lord Jesus Christ, I give you my whole life now. Please come and live in my heart. Wash away all my sins. Fill me with your Holy Spirit. Thank you that you will never leave me.

After they have prayed, I would pray an immediate prayer of thanks, asking God to bless and keep his new child. Then I would give them a hug (if appropriate!) and a verse of assurance – something appropriate, which might be John 6:37, John 10:28, Hebrews 13:5 ('Never will I leave you; never will I forsake you'), or Revelation 3:20 ('I will come in').

It may help if they tell you what they have done. If they are thrilled, help them to see that it is all of Jesus, so when they do *not* feel on cloud nine they know he is still there. If they say they feel nothing, explain that it is not about feelings but about trusting someone who is telling the whole truth when he says, 'I will come in.'

For yourself, remember this is only the beginning. Arrange to meet again very soon, and hurry on to Key 8 to see what you need to do now.

Key 8: From Here to Eternity

Here is a serious observation: if you won't do what this key says then don't bother with the first seven keys. No baby should ever be conceived who will not be cared for when they come into the world. When a person is 'born again', an expression first used by Jesus himself to explain the new life he gives (John 3:3), they are brand new as a Christian. If you are unable to care for this new spiritual baby, what plans do you have for their care? Work this out before Key 2.

You do not necessarily have to meet all the following needs. Your church leader and fellow members should be in there with you. But any new Christian will need help in all these.

Assurance

We have looked at this at the end of Key 7, because it is needed immediately someone has trusted Christ as their Saviour and Lord. John wrote to his Christian friends in order that, 'You may know that you have eternal life' (1 John 5:13). Give a verse of certainty. John 6:37 is excellent: 'Whoever comes to me I will never drive away.'

Make sure they are sure.

Prayer and the Bible

Being a Christian means, above all, a personal relationship with God as our Father, through his Son Jesus and by the power of the Holy Spirit. This intimate relationship is a two-way, one-to-one family friendship. For it to develop in this way, two things will prove vital at a personal level.

One is prayer. Share how you pray and what you pray about. Long ago they used to say that prayer was Adoration, Confession, Thanksgiving and Supplication (A.C.T.S.). Those were big words, but not too bad a guide. The idea to get across is that we can pray about anything and anyone, anywhere and at any time. However, a time specifically set aside each day will prove very worthwhile. Offer to spend a time each week with the new Christian to pray with them.

The second is listening to God and hearing from him. This is done by learning to recognise the voice of the Holy Spirit and allowing the fruit of this Spirit to grow in our lives (Galatians 5: 22–23). God's way and will is most clearly spelt out in his word, the Bible. Explain how the Bible helps your Christian life, and advise how it is best read. Say that Mark's Gospel is a good place to start, rather than Leviticus. Romans might follow, some considerable time before Job.

All babies gradually learn to feed. So do new Christians! 'Like new born babies, crave pure spiritual milk, so that you may grow up in your salvation' (1 Peter 2:2). They may well appreciate some good Bible reading notes: Scripture Union and CWR (*Every Day With Jesus*) can help here. You could make time to read the Bible together once a week, and for you to field any questions – even if you don't know all the answers!

Fellowship

It is wonderful to be Christians together! Does your church have a nurture group for new Christians? Are you a member of a home group or a 'cell'? When does your Christian group get together? We learn to play this game of life in small teams. Bring your friend into your group, and make sure your team makes them welcome, so that they feel at home and able to cope. This may be much more helpful than church, though we will come to that directly. Remember 'the fellowship of the Holy Spirit' (2 Corinthians 13:14). His is the best friendship of all. We want every Christian to 'be filled with the Spirit' (Ephesians 5:18).

Church

Church is a great place to be a Christian, and to grow in the faith, if you have some idea of what on earth is going on. Most people today only see the inside of a church at a wedding or a funeral, so the Sunday service is completely alien. You and I enjoy it, because we are part of the mystique. If your new Christian is to survive and get to the enjoyment level, they need your help.

Explain what is likely to happen, and why. Say who will do what, and how the congregation fits in. Laugh about the fact that some of the worship is not entirely your scene, and that some songs are new even to you. If various gifts could be evident, show from the Bible (as in 1 Corinthians 12–14) what they mean.

Church is for all Christians. 'Let us not give up meeting together' (Hebrews 10:25). We are to 'speak to one another with psalms, hymns and spiritual songs' (Ephesians 5:19). Bring the new Christian into the family of the church, with lots of help as you sit alongside them, taking away the panic factor of a strange new environment.

Witnessing

The story at the beginning of Key 5 is relevant here. You will need the Holy Spirit's wisdom as you advise your new

Christian as to the most appropriate ways to share their new faith with others. Standing on the proverbial soapbox outside the office and preaching may not be the best idea. A quiet word with the office gossip will work just as well, and probably faster. A loving style at home will help, but a condemnation of every sinner in sight may prove counter-productive.

You will realise that, whether you fancy the idea or not, you will be in an advisory capacity. Unless they are getting things hopelessly wrong, it is better to respond to questions than lay down too many ground rules. Do help them to speak up as well as shut up as new Christians. Their new story is worth hearing.

Friendship

If you forget all the rest, grab hold of this one. A new Christian needs your friendship more than anything else you can give. God can do the rest! But he wants you to be a brother or sister to one of his new children. You can do it. This is the key to Key 8.

The 50

The Stats

One of the dangers in writing a book like this is answering the questions no one is asking. So the 40:3 Trust for whom I work did a survey of nearly 200 people, asking the question, 'Who would I like to help become a Christian?' Here is a pie chart breakdown of their responses:

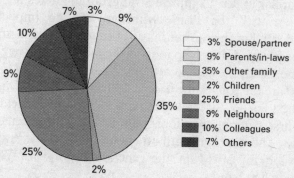

Chart 4: Who would I like to help become a Christian?

3%	Spouse/partner
9%	Parents/in-laws
35%	Other family
2%	Children
25%	Friends
9%	Neighbours
10%	Colleagues
7%	Others

Some of these are predictable, others surprising. In our concerns for our families, have we forgotten our neighbours? We seem much more interested in our friends than the people with whom we work. Or is all this unfair, as only one answer could be given? If more than one 'vote' were possible, who would have come second? In the end I decided every category was important, and every person mentioned in replies will be included in 'The 50'.

Some are obvious, especially the almost 50 per cent under the heading 'Family', and a further pie chart will show later a breakdown in that section. Others have given me cause to do some head-scratching. How do you share your faith with 'the roof man'? Climb up his ladder for a chat? I will include him under 'Neighbours: Outside Helpers'. What about 'the Prime Minister'? Could a trip be arranged to Downing Street, London? He comes under 'Complete Strangers'. 'The bouncer' will find a place in 'Acquaintances: Clubbers'. 'At Work: The Daily Journey' will try to help the person who replied 'the taxi driver'.

I am stumped by one response to 'Who would I like to help become a Christian?' Answer: 'the burglar'. Ah, right. I know what you mean. But it is rather like the first instruction in the cookery book, under the heading 'How to cook a wild pig', which reads, 'First catch your wild pig.' I will include the burglar under 'Complete Strangers' (an interesting combination with the Prime Minister, and no implication intended!), but the answer may not be totally satisfactory.

The person I may help most is the one who answered the question with the simple response 'anyone'. All the following 50 are for you! Some people, instead of saying 'Dad', or 'my best friend', had a wider request, such as 'the elderly'. Our first section, therefore, puts people into specific categories, and may help with others who follow. For example, when looking at 'Mum' the general category of 'Women' may come in handy.

1 Men

Please forgive the implied sexism, but someone had to come first, and everyone seems agreed that it would be great to have loads more men as Christians.

To share our faith with anyone, whoever they are, we need to try to understand them. In the last few decades there seems to have been a particular move away from God by men. But in very recent days I have detected a small but significant move back by some men, so I am looking at this first category with optimism.

Men on the outside

Do you remember the early days of Simon and Garfunkel? Their song 'I am a rock' included the words, 'I've built walls, a fortress deep and mighty, that none may penetrate.' The problem for faith-sharing with men is getting through the 'walls'. Four such barriers are:

- *Pride.* Men often want to be Numero Uno, the leader of the pack, with the motto, 'I did it my way.' We shall meet this under 'Husband'.
- *Fear.* The male disciples ran away, but the women stayed by the cross. Often, men are afraid they might have to stand alone as Christians, and the cost would be too much.
- *Ignorance.* Many men know little of God, his love, his way and his life. God is irrelevant to vast numbers of men.

- *Sin.* Men are much more obvious sinners than women! There would be so much that men would need to leave behind if Jesus brought change.

How can these barriers be broken down?

Changed men

The negatives which keep men on the outside are counter-balanced by a set of positives to help them come in.

- *Vision.* Men may be too proud to bow to anyone, but the greatness of Jesus means he alone deserves honour. Church, Christians, even worship may be off-putting. But Jesus himself is a 'man's man', the great rock who is 'higher than I' (Psalm 61:2). There is no shame in coming to acknowledge this 'rock of ages'; the 'cornerstone' (1 Peter 2:6) to build a new life on. Take men to Jesus; to his cross where men's sin is dealt with; to his resurrection where his power is seen; to Pentecost, where his power is received. A wishy-washy, watery, toned-down vision will not do.
- *Attitude.* Check out the 'men of faith' in Hebrews 11, and show how they did not start like that. They were ordinary doubters, cowards, failures, sinners and nobodies, made great by God. He took their fear.
- *Life.* Men do not want rules and regulations: they want life. Back to the 'rock' theme: 'With honey from the rock I would satisfy you' (Psalm 81:16). The dynamic, challenging life through a relationship with Jesus appeals to men.

What can be done?

- *Don't threaten*: defences will come up.
- *Be interested in him as a person.* Most people are only

concerned with what he does (at work, at home, at sport, even at church): he is someone (Key 2).

- *Be a real friend*: men have few genuine friends.
- It is almost invariably better *man-to-man*. A woman's approach could well be misconstrued for all sorts of different reasons – beware!
- *Be direct*. Men don't like beating about the bush. Talk about Jesus and the personal relationship you enjoy (Key 3). Go to him. He will feel more comfortable in his pub/club/sports centre than in your church, which will be alien territory.
- *Get your church 'man-thinking'*. There is so much for couples, children, families, women, older people and the musical: where is the man-orientation? An occasional men-only event may well attract men from outside, especially when food and drink are involved. Don't be afraid to have a good Christian (male) speaker.
- *Have a long-term strategy*, softly-softly. He may well have a considerable way to come.
- If you must invite him to a church service, *check it out beforehand* with your leaders. You don't want 'twee', soppy songs, 'in' language, complicated liturgies or anything which will make an outside man stick out like a sore thumb. Songs pitched not too high, a simple direct talk and a happy atmosphere will work wonders.
- Never forget Key 3's advice on *prayer*. God loves and wants that man. In prayer, listen for God's leading. He has a plan for reaching him. Does it involve you?

2 Women

Women are different from men. There is no exclamation mark at the end of that sentence: it is a fact. This chapter will not, therefore, be comparable with the last one, but some contrasts will appear.

What women want

There are certain sections of this book where I am, obviously, not one of the people concerned, and no more so than here. However, in *100 Faith-Sharing Talks* (Kingsway), I outlined some of the positives which could be included in a talk to women, and they are germane here.

- *Truth.* Women get tired of being conned, whether it be by men and their 'promises, promises', or by supermarkets and their gimmicks. Even more than men do, women want to know if the faith we share is real. The good news is, not only is Christianity real but the Bible's women are the witnesses. Mary, the mother of Jesus, knew more about the virgin birth than any bishop (Luke 1:31–35). Martha believed the words of Jesus that he is 'the resurrection and the life' (John 11:25) before her brother Lazarus was raised, and before the crucifixion and resurrection. Christianity is no 'con', and its reality in your life will ring bells.
- *Triumph.* Women are quicker than men at appreciating that Jesus brings victory in life. Again, New Testament women are the key here. The women saw Jesus defeat sin

by his death on the cross, after the men were long gone (Mark 15:40). One was even the mother of a hiding disciple. Similarly, the women came first to the tomb (Matthew 28:1), and a woman, 'Mary' (John 20:18), with another Mary (Matthew 28:8), announced the resurrection victory. Bearing in mind that, in those days, a woman was not allowed to give evidence in court, it is a startling way for God to speak to the first post-resurrection people, apparently an all-male audience. Here again, it will help in faith-sharing with a woman to show that Christianity is not only true, but works and wins.

- *Time.* Why is it women often seem closer to God and appear more faithful in prayer? Ask any Christian worker: the vast majority of their prayer partners are female. It is because women are willing, in their very busy lives, to give quality time to Jesus. It is helpful to show that Jesus always has time for women. The story of the woman at the well in John 4:4–42 is a supreme example of Jesus ignoring convention to spend a long time with one foreign, not-so-good, 'outsider'. Conversely, the famous home visit to Martha and Mary (Luke 10:38–42) shows how our time is valuable to Jesus. Jesus wants to be involved in our lives, and vice versa. This can be presented as a privilege, not a burden, because of how wonderful he is and the blessings which follow.

- *Treasure and tears.* The costliness of knowing Jesus is another feature of Christianity which will impact women. The woman who gave the expensive ointment for Jesus is mentioned in all four Gospels (Matthew 26:6–13; Mark 14:3–9; Luke 7: 37–50; John 12:1–8). It is the women who weep as Jesus goes to be crucified (Luke 23:27–28). But women rise to this challenge, facing the cost of following Jesus much better than men.

- *Trust.* Perhaps the best way of all to faith-share with a woman is to speak of the wonderful relationship she will come into in knowing Jesus. Your own testimony (Key 3) should reflect this. Jesus brings new life, as in the mother-in-law incident (Mark 1:29–31). Women were able to trust Jesus with their children (Mark 10:13–16), including when those children were ill (Mark 7:24–30). This one-to-one knowing Jesus, and being able to trust him with ourselves, our families and our concerns, matters to women.

Some practicalities

- As with the chapter on men, same-sex conversations are not only safer but will work much better. After all, a woman can never be sure of a man's motives. And again, how can he understand? What does he know?
- A woman will appreciate a relaxed situation and an easy-going style. She will back away from aggression, and will want to talk at a time when she is not under pressure from the many demands on her life.
- Friendship is crucial, much more than for a man.
- Laughter works wonders!

3 Children

We have just seen, when looking at women and their concern for their families, the attitude of Jesus to children. When others wanted them to stay away, he welcomed them and blessed them (Mark 10:13–16). They were included in his healing ministry (Mark 7:24–30; Matthew 17:14–18). We can and should share our faith with children.

I am personally very biased here. I look back to the age of seven as the time when my own Christian life started. One Sunday afternoon I went with my mother and younger siblings to the centre of our town. The Salvation Army band was playing by the town clock. In between hymns, a teenage girl in the Army said one sentence which touched my heart: 'You need Jesus to be your Saviour.' As we walked home, I said to my mother, 'I want Jesus to be my Saviour.' 'Then when we get home, you must ask him,' was her reply. And I did. It is more than 50 years from that day, but I remember it as yesterday.

From my own experience and with a lot of help from someone who has studied this area in depth – Penny Frank – here are some pointers.

How to faith-share with children

- Realise more than anything that God loves children. They are his examples of what the kingdom of heaven is like: we have to become like them, not them like us (Matthew 18:1–4).
- Let them come to Jesus when he calls them, not when you think it is a good idea (this is true about everyone, of

77

course). My parents were both Christians and would have been praying for me. But it was when I heard God's voice through an 'outsider' that I was ready.

- Under absolutely no circumstances should any pressure whatsoever be exerted. (Have I put that strongly enough?!) Even after I had heard of my need, my mother waited for my response, and only then gave me the opportunity to respond, with some more thinking time before we got home.
- Children have determination and therefore will respond if they really want to. I was always helped on this by the very fine children's evangelists Ralph Chambers and Irene Wardle (Children's Christian Crusade). At the end of a week's meetings for children, the boys and girls were asked to leave the last meeting, only returning if they wanted to talk further about trusting Christ. They had to take a deliberate step to do so.
- Never offer a prize or reward. In a meeting, the chance to receive a booklet may get a wrong response unless very carefully handled.
- Be gentle: here is a tender heart.
- Be honest. Children at school may have the hardest time of anyone in having to stand out as Christians.
- Be natural. Faith-sharing with children is often best accompanied by your engaging in their activities, and caring about them as people.
- Be simple, but not simplistic. It is my experience that children can understand very deep spiritual things, as long as they are explained in a style they can relate to. As one example, that greatest of all children's evangelists, Richard Hudson-Pope, was once asked by a child, 'What does it mean to "be filled with the Spirit"?' He replied: 'It means that your life is so full of Jesus that, when the devil knocks on the door, you look out from your top window and shout down to him, "I'm sorry, we're full up here."' Brilliant!

What to say

Penny Frank, when lecturing to the Birmingham Bible Institute, took an interesting, unusual and extremely helpful line here. She drew on Exodus 13:1-16. Her main points (with my embellishments) were these:

- When the Israelites told their children of the exodus (verse 14), it was a great story of God at work.
- It was what God had said (verse 9), not a jolly little story made up for the occasion.
- It was what God had done (the rescue in verses 14-15).
- It showed who they themselves were (verses 2, 12, 15).
- It was a very important story, to do with personal faith, national pride and their family life. I sometimes wonder if we tell some Bible stories because they are just good stories, but really they have little significance and so make no impact on the real life of a child.

Penny went on to relate this deliverance by God of the Israelites from Egypt to the rescue Jesus brought for us at the cross. The redemption from Egypt is not a national tale for most children, but it prepares for the tale of the cross. That also contains what God has said and done, who we are, and is of supreme importance. My own story is that, whatever stories I had heard from my parents and in Sunday school, it was Jesus wanting to be my Saviour that spoke to my heart.

Penny's final advice would be mine too: pray! I would add, check out Key 8 especially: looking after a child who has trusted Jesus is mega-important.

4 Teenagers

This category received one solitary reply in our survey about faith-sharing. That's all. The answer simply said 'the village youth' – which I took to mean several people, not just one teenager. Perhaps this reflects the lack of concern we have for others, but I believe our young people urgently need to find a real faith in Jesus Christ. Interestingly, some answers revealed that people want the *church* to reach out to teenagers.

The teenage world

Whole books have failed to describe the world of the teenager, because of its contradictions. While a boy may be 15 going on seven, his female counterpart could be 13 going on 25, with an occasional tantrum of a three-year-old. The problem is, everything happens at the same time: greater responsibility and accountability, puberty, awkwardness and embarrassment, owning or jettisoning faith, escaping from parents and discovering the opposite sex, being an individual and yet 'one of the crowd'. If you are not in your teens, you may try hard to remember and understand, but you will never be one of them. My 16-year-old wrote in his 24-year-old brother's birthday card, 'Welcome to old age.'

You want to faith-share with a teenager? Here are a few tentative suggestions (once again with help from Mike Coe, my former youth evangelist-turned-clergyman).

The don'ts

'Young people today love luxury. They have dreadful manners, contempt for authority and no respect for older people. What sort of awful creatures will they be when they grow up?' Good old Socrates! This fourth-century Greek philosopher is our guide to the first 'don't'. Lay off the criticism – the idea that God will help to improve their behaviour is anathema to the true meaning of the good news.

Next, you don't have to be like them. One of my teenagers (our family has enjoyed four) uses the word 'cool' to signify anything which is not only OK but part of his culture. I foolishly asked one day if I were cool. He gave me what could best be described as a kindly, pitying look, and replied, 'You're not cool – you're my *dad*.' To confuse me completely, when I told him I was writing this about him in this book, he replied, 'Cool.' I think I see. . . .

Don't compare it with 'when I was young'. As American comedian Bill Cosby says, 'You were never young. You were old in the womb!'

Enough negatives! There are some real positives.

The do's

- Be a friend (we've met this one before – is the penny dropping?). Anyone of any age can do this, and a big generational gap may be especially effective.
- Your own failures when younger will go down better than your successes. Try not to exaggerate!
- Have your own consistent standards: hypocrisy will be spotted at once. Teenagers often prove that 'Christianity is caught, not taught'.
- Encourage other teenagers to help (Key 5). The best people to reach teenagers are teenagers.

- Surprisingly perhaps, this age group can react well to good Christian gatherings, and respond to Christ there.
- Be willing to answer big, tough questions honestly. This is the 'Why' age. The answer 'I don't know' is perfectly legitimate.
- Make your teenager feel special, and loved. Value him or her. The world around sees them as 'a market' or 'exam fodder'. MTV's Ben Johnson said, 'We don't influence 11- to 14-year-olds: we own them.'
- Give them space to discover Jesus Christ. Remember, James and John were almost certainly teenagers fishing from their dad's boat when Jesus called them (Mark 1:19–20). He wants teenagers on his 'front line' today, so you have no need to push.
- Conversely, you may have to make the moves. They may not feel able to approach you in the first place.
- They will appreciate straight talk. They rise to a challenge. Wishy-washy Christianity will be seen for what it is, and rejected.

A final thought

As I have already mentioned, a 1997 opinion poll found that 87 per cent of all young people had no contact with God at all. Whoever else we want to share our faith with, will we fail this young generation?

5 Generation X

We are moving slowly through the age groups, having now reached those described by Douglas Coupland in his book *Generation X: Tales of an Accelerated Culture* as those born between 1961 and 1981. This 'Generation X', he says, does not know who it is and has no real focus or hope for the future. Again, Mike Coe is my helper–guide here. (You will realise I am on another 'thank you', with more to come. I am not the fount of all knowledge on faith-sharing, so don't fret if you are not, either.)

I am looking now at young adults moving towards middle-age. This is the group born into what is called the 'postmodern era', characterised by major moves from previous standards of belief in society, as will now be seen.

Some problems

- *Truth has gone.* 'What is truth?' Pilate asked Jesus (John 18:38), but went out before the answer. Generation X has no absolutes. Even what is seen cannot be believed; it has to be experienced.
- *Love has gone* – at least, it has for many. This generation has a one in two divorce rate, many now refuse to get married, and lifelong relationships seem impossible. Pressures on family life have increased greatly.
- *Security has gone.* A 'job for life' does not exist any more. Redundancies are the norm. Rules like the Ten Commandments have been abandoned, so there are no absolute standards.

- *Purpose has gone*. There is a pervading hopelessness and a mistrust in everyone.
- I do not know who, or why, I am. I am what I do. The joke goes like this. It is no longer 'I think, therefore I am' – '*Cogito, ergo sum*' (Descartes). Now it is: 'I play, therefore I am' (*ludo ergo sum*); 'I shop, therefore I am' (*Tesco ergo sum*); 'I drink, therefore I am' (*vino ergo sum*) – and so on.
- Major influences on the lives of this generation include:
  - TV, films and videos, moulding minds. By the age of 25, most people have seen some 250,000 adverts. These adverts say that style wins over substance.
  - Shopping. The 'god' of Sundays, shopping is now a leisure pursuit, with malls replacing churches. It is the 'image' of the product which is everything.
  - Tolerance must rule, at all costs, with diversity and vast choices welcomed.
  - The feel-good factor. If it feels good to me, it's OK. Everything is subjective; absolutes (like Christianity) are 'out'. This is the essence of postmodernity.
  - The 'pop' culture is to be revered. *Hello* magazine is the iconic Bible.

Some answers

If you want to share your faith with those in their twenties, thirties and early forties, here are a few ideas.

- They are almost certainly not aware of the subtle influences just mentioned, nor of the impact on their society and their own lives. Take the above as read and don't argue against them. One of postmodernism's strengths is that it is like trying to nail jelly to a wall. It has been described as 'something and nothing', and is not an organised movement. Its value for us is that it does not need to be argued against, as communism did, for example.

- There has been a shift from emphasising absolute truth to subjective reality. Does what we are saying about Jesus work? Your testimony (Key 3) becomes crucial. Because 'Jesus Christ is the same yesterday and today and for ever' (Hebrews 13:8), it is not surprising that he has the answer for this 'feeling' generation. For an older generation, he is the absolute: 'I am the way and the truth and the life' (John 14:6). For Generation X, Jesus offers to meet all those 'feeling' needs: joy (John 15:11); peace (John 14:27); comfort (Isaiah 40:1); and the various qualities in the fruit of the Spirit detailed in Galatians 5:22–23. Their needs are all met in him.

- With the fragmentation of society, and the uncertainty of such basics as marriage, family and work, the Christian community stands out as a beacon of hope and life. It must diversify, so church is not the sole venue, but it is a major way to reach Generation X.

- The reality of your own experience of knowing Jesus does not mean you have to be impossibly perfect. Your honesty about failures as a Christian, as well as God's successes in you, will count for a lot.

Final suggestions

On a personal note, I have found the reality of God's forgiveness rings bells with this group. His love, in a loveless world, is a precious gift to be received. The one-to-one or couple-to-couple approach may be time-consuming, but it will probably prove the most effective here. Those within Generation X need to reach their contemporaries.

6 New Agers

Our journey through the generations must include those subject to the 'New Age' culture. Although this includes many in Generation X, it takes in an older generation. For example, one of the so-called 'high priestesses' of the New Age culture is actress Shirley Maclaine, born in 1934. An understanding of the last chapter, especially the bits about postmodernism, will help.

What is New Age?

Like postmodernism, 'New Age' is in the 'nailing jelly to the wall' category. It is a mix 'n' match of various spiritual notions to replace Christianity, heralding the 'Age of Aquarius', transforming planet Earth and its inhabitants, bringing in a 'New Age' of love, peace and light. I'm afraid I remember the tongue-in-cheek definition of Aquarians by the late Michael Flanders (of Flanders and Swann) as 'the ones who carry the can' (Aquarius being the water-carrier).

The perpetrators of New Age must, indeed, carry the can for the confusion caused. Its followers are encouraged to abandon any ultimate truth for 'what's true for you'. Ignorance is an obstacle (good), but so is narrow-minded-ness, which automatically excludes the restrictive, irrelevant and intolerable Christianity. Thus the tolerance of New Age is intolerant of Christians. Interesting. 'God' is a higher 'life force'; 'Mother Earth', a god-in-you – but certainly neither personal nor transcendent. What is inside you is what matters, and your experience proves something is real, because 'it works'. Within New Age are some beliefs gleaned from Eastern religions. The occult plays quite a role, with beliefs in the power within certain rocks, for example.

Of course, you can pick and choose the bits for you, as long as they work for you and providing you exclude all absolutes. If you hear an echo of the chaos at the end of Judges you are right: 'In those days Israel had no king; everyone did as he saw fit' (Judges 21: 25). The Preacher was right, 'There is nothing new under the sun' (Ecclesiastes 1:9).

Some relevant questions

Apart from the famous, such as Shirley Maclaine, does the average person know what they are into in New Age? Is God really just a soulless force? Is Jesus just a great moral teacher? Do all roads lead to God? What is the 'Life Force'? Why *did* Jesus die? What do we think about during meditation? Is there any proof of reincarnation? Is there any evidence that we are getting better as people?

You see the problems New Agers have? And these are just some of them! The best they can do is to hope. And that hope is, ultimately, in something within themselves. It is a desperate attempt to find a substitute for the challenges of Christianity. How can we help with our faith?

- This world of the New Age serves to confuse. We all want to get our minds working the right way: 'Do not conform any longer to the pattern of this world, but be transformed by the renewing of your mind' (Romans 12:2). Share how amazing it is to experience that 'we have the mind of Christ' (1 Corinthians 2:16).
- We all long for freedom – a real 'New Age'. The wrong within us entraps us from reaching it (John 8:34), but 'if the Son sets you free, you will be free indeed' (John 8:36).
- Christians are genuinely concerned for the well being of

the world: they have been at the forefront of this, and New Agers alone cannot take the credit.

• We all want to know if what we believe is true, not just a good idea. Jesus said, 'If you hold to my teaching, you are really my disciples. Then you will know the truth, and the truth will set you free' (John 8:32).

• If we are looking for a 'New Age', check out the last two chapters of the Bible: sensational!

Remember, you may know more about 'New Age' ideas than its adherents. Share the wonder of being sure of what you believe in Jesus. It is safer to believe in his reality than in a piece of rock bought in a New Age shop. This personal, loving relationship with Jesus is the best way to help New Agers.

7 Older People

In all the replies to the question about 'the person with whom I would like to share my faith', only one person mentioned the older generations. I am personally involved in evangelism throughout the United Kingdom, and I find very few churches think about reaching out to older people.

This is a huge mistake to make! The world is filling up with older people, and 50 per cent of all voters are now aged over 50. This may be the last time we will have people around who have a background knowledge of the Bible: remember the earlier statistic that over 80 per cent of the population said they had been to Sunday school when asked in a 1955 opinion poll.

'Older people' is better than 'elderly' as a term. When does it begin? The latest figures start at 55 (Saga holidays start at 50). When you were 21, when did you think 'old' started? I put it, when I was 21, at 40. Only when I reached that age did I realise how young 40 was. This is not a 'debate of the age', but about faith-sharing. Having made your hackles rise if you are 55, let's look at sharing our faith with older people.

The problems

- It is hard to change as you grow old: 'You can't teach an old dog new tricks.' We want continuity, not a radical change of life and lifestyle.
- It is hard to admit that a lifetime of beliefs (or non-beliefs) was wrong. This is the generation that says, 'I did my best,'

'I did it my way,' 'I never did anybody any harm,' 'I'm as good as the next.'
- It is hard to live with an increasing lack of mobility, and an increase in loneliness, bereavement and ageing itself.
- It is hard to face death, and easier to avoid thinking about it.

The pitfalls

There are three things to remember when getting involved with older people:

- Don't try to show you 'understand'. How can you, if you are much younger? On the other hand, if you are older yourself, you are the ideal person to share your faith with your peers: that's why evangelism has no retirement date.
- Don't underestimate an older person's intelligence. They probably know more than you do. They may even know more of the Bible, with a Sunday school and church background.
- Don't patronise. We tend to speak to very old people as if they were children, which is insulting.

The potential

With nearly a quarter of the population over 60, here is a potential army of older followers of Jesus Christ. Their lives could influence, and even change, the whole nation. Here would be the living proof of a future and a hope. Robert Browning, in his poem 'Rabbi ben Ezra', wrote:

> Grow old along with me!
> The best is yet to be,
> The last of life, for which the first was made.

> Our times are in His hand
> Who saith, 'A whole I planned.
> Youth shows but half; trust God:
> See all nor be afraid!'

Browning is right: the older years should be ones of fulfilment, and the prospect of growing older with Jesus is wonderful. Link with this a life forgiven, peace with God and a future in heaven, and don't you get excited about sharing this faith with an older person?

The plan

More than with almost anyone else, friendship is the answer here (Key 2). Love and respect are vital. Even family members have little time for older members.

Here are four suggestions on how to approach faith-sharing with an older person:

- Speak of their potential. When David says 'I was young and now I am old' (Psalm 37:25), his words are interpreted today to mean 'I'm useless', 'I'm forgotten', 'I'm hopeless'. God says otherwise. He speaks of being with us in our 'old age' and with our 'grey hairs' (Isaiah 46:4), helping and keeping us. His plan is for us to 'still bear fruit in old age', staying 'fresh and green' (Psalm 92:14), echoed in Browning's words.
- Speak of God's love for older ones and his respect for old age. The Bible is full of amazing stories of God using older people in his plans: Moses, Caleb, Anna and Simeon, Abraham and Sarah, Zechariah and Elizabeth – the list goes on.
- John 3 is a passage for older people: Nicodemus is, on his own admission, 'old' (verse 4). John 3:16 is for older people! Jesus gives new lives for old.

- Eternity, and its answer to death, is a great subject for an older person. They may well know the first few verses of John 14 by heart. I sat with an old man, a neighbour, and started to read, 'Do not let your hearts be troubled . . .' (verse 1). I was amazed as he recited along with me right up to verse 6. It was so easy to talk about heaven with him. He trusted Christ as a result – and died a fortnight later.

In all your faith-sharing, do include the older ones.

8 The Bereaved

Billy Graham once said, 'As I grow older, I seem to go to more funerals.' Although bereavement comes to all ages, I have put this chapter after the one about older people because the two often overlap. However, it will apply to anyone who is bereaved. My style of approach adopted here is the same as the last chapter.

The problems

Bereavement is very often, in itself, life-changing. In my book *Bereaved – Coping with Loss* (Kingsway), I listed the following major problems as being both typical and normal when someone is bereaved:

- *Shock and disbelief*, especially if the death is sudden and unexpected.
- *Anger and darkness*. 'Why has God let this happen?' This is the dark 'valley of the shadow of death' (Psalm 23:4).
- *Depression*. The feeling of being 'down'.
- *Loneliness*. This is very hard, because the person is not coming back to relieve the loneliness.
- *Lostness*. 'What's the point of living now they are gone?' 'Where am I going now?'
- *Guilt*. Bereavement often brings 'if onlys': 'If only I'd said "sorry",' 'If only I'd said "goodbye",' 'If only I'd said "I love you".'

The pitfalls

This is a very sensitive time, and helping someone who is bereaved needs to be handled with great care, or faith-sharing will produce a negative response. Here are four areas to watch:

- Beware the danger of avoidance. It is easier to keep away from a bereaved person because we do not know what to say. A friend of mine gave birth to a badly deformed daughter, and so was 'bereaved' of the child she wanted. She told me the most hurtful thing was to see a Christian friend cross over the road to avoid meeting her. Company was what she wanted.
- Do not say too much. A bereaved person is very vulnerable, and does not need a sermon.
- Avoid over-spirituality. Trite 'spiritual' answers will be very counter-productive. Practical help is much to be preferred (what about making a hot meal, or going with the bereaved person when they have to register the death, or helping with the shopping?).
- Most of all, there is the danger of no 'heart' concern. Love, care and even tears are needed. Don't force the latter, but don't be too big to cry when the bereaved person does, if you are so moved.

The potential

The possibilities of positive progress are enormous here, given time and care.

- Here is the chance for you to share the burden, and to see it handed over to Jesus, who cares (1 Peter 5:7).
- There is God's help, and hope, in the midst of bereavement: in the valley of death, 'I will fear no evil, for you are with me' (Psalm 23:4).

- Jesus is the light both in and at the end of the tunnel: 'I am the light of the world,' he said. 'Whoever follows me will never walk in darkness, but will have the light of life' (John 8:12).
- According to recent research, 13 per cent of all those who become Christians say they did so at a time of bereavement or loss. Bereaved people are not all waving their fists at God; some are looking to him for help.
- Faith-sharing can, therefore, lead to that lovely word 'salvation', with its meaning of health, wholeness and completeness in Jesus. It was to a bereaved person (Martha) that Jesus said the opening words of the funeral service: 'I am the resurrection and the life. He who believes in me will live, even though he dies; and whoever lives and believes in me will never die' (John 11:25). Jesus then immediately asked this just-bereaved woman, 'Do you believe this?' And she did!

The plan

When I faith-share with a bereaved person, I am keenly aware of finding the right time (Key 4) and being enormously sensitive (Keys 6 and 7). I would have three things in mind, which may be mutually inclusive of each other.

First, I would want to take a bereaved person to what God says in the Bible, perhaps sooner than any other person. We have already touched on Psalm 23, perhaps the ideal scripture here. Martha's experience is followed by the Bible's shortest verse, 'Jesus wept' (John 11:35). Wherever you have found comfort in God's word, use that to show how God has helped you at times of sorrow and crisis.

Next, I would want to take a bereaved person to the cross of Jesus Christ. It was there that God the Father was himself bereaved, and the very sky turned dark at noon (Luke 23:44–45) with heaven's sorrow and grief. Isaiah 53 is the greatest Old Testament passage on the cross, and includes those wonderful words of comfort and hope about Jesus: 'Surely he took up our infirmities and carried our sorrows' (verse 4). God both understands our bereavements and has carried the pain of them.

Finally, I would (with great gentleness) show how it is at this time especially that Jesus makes his invitation for us to respond to him. Look at his remarkable words: 'Come to me, all you who are weary and burdened, and I will give you rest . . . you will find rest for your souls' (Matthew 11:28–29).

Don't back away from the bereaved. They are precious people with whom we can share our faith.

9   Other Faiths

Many of us, in our multiracial society, have neighbours, friends, work colleagues and sometimes family members who belong to other faiths. What about faith-sharing with them? Should we? Could we? Can we? Shall we?

Observant readers will notice that the letter 'P' is very handy for headings, and four more apply here – though not all the same as in the previous two chapters.

The principle

I read in one dreadful misinterpretation of the beginning of John 3:16: 'God so loved the elect.' No! No! No! 'God so loved the *world*.' We Christians do not have an exclusive hold on the love of God nor the right to believe that 'he gave his one and only Son' just for us. It was for 'whoever'. In days of deep racial prejudice, we are to 'go and make disciples of all nations' (Matthew 28:19).

The principle is stated very clearly in the last words of Jesus before his ascension:

'You will receive power when the Holy Spirit comes on you: and you will be my witnesses in Jerusalem, and in all Judea and Samaria, and to the ends of the earth.' (Acts 1:8)

There was to be no limitation on faith-sharing by the 'witnesses'. Whoever was living in multicultural Jerusalem was included. The Jews may have been racially prejudiced about the Samaritans, but they are there in the list. 'The ends of the

97

earth' meant every race, colour and creed then, and still does today. We happen to be especially fortunate, because 'the ends of the earth' have now come to us, living and working alongside us. I go to a church which regularly has 15 or 20 nationalities represented, with a technicolour of hues, from a variety of other-faith backgrounds.

The principle is clear: God loves everyone, whatever their faith, and sends us to share our faith with them.

Some problems

The easiest thing, in talking with a member of another faith, is to get into an argument about who, or which, is right. How can this be avoided?

First, it may be appropriate to apologise for the many times dreadful things have been done in the name of Christianity. Many of them were political gaffes, even though done in the name of Christ. The medieval Crusades caused untold suffering and long-term enmity towards Christians by Jews and Muslims. The over-zealous colonisation of India and Africa left millions resenting the overbearing 'Christian' West, including the various faiths in the Indian subcontinent and the tribal religions of Africa. The Roman Catholic Irish were treated disgracefully in previous centuries, making faith-sharing today difficult. The list goes on, and would include some churches' attitude at the time to the Holocaust killings of millions of Jews.

These indefensible actions can only be met with a genuine and heartfelt sorrow on our part and, if possible, an explanation that they are a travesty of the way Jesus behaved. Quite a lot of repair work is needed with many members of other faiths.

Second, two features of Jesus can be misconstrued, and can become insurmountable barriers. Some faiths believe in the single oneness of God (the Muslims especially). Speaking of Jesus as 'God', or 'the Son of God', will not be helpful at an early stage. It is better to talk of his life and to see him as 'Saviour' first. Unfortunately this causes a further problem, as the Koran denies the death of Jesus, so the cross itself also needs to be approached with care.

Positives

Mark Beaumont, Deputy Principal of the Birmingham Christian College, has helped me greatly here by suggesting five matters which are of particular value in faith-sharing with members of other religions.

1. *Jesus.* Other faiths may not like our religion, but they are hugely attracted to Jesus. They like him. Show them his character, what he is like and what he does. Start where the Gospels do – at the beginning. Even the disciples came slowly, and with both difficulty and objections, to the crucifixion.
2. *Forgiveness.* God's forgiveness through Jesus is a unique feature. No other religion has an overall certainty of our being forgiven by a holy God. The incident in Mark 2:1–12, when Jesus forgives the paralysed man before healing him, is very intriguing to those whose faith has little to say about forgiveness.
3. *Grace.* The undeserved love of God towards us is a major attraction. The story of Zacchaeus (Luke 19:1–10), or the woman taken in adultery (John 8:1–11), or the prodigal son (Luke 15:11–32) would be good. It is the way God takes the initiative which appeals. Muhammad retired to a cave in search of God. But God came to choose Abraham (Genesis 12:1), Gideon (Judges 6:11–12), Isaiah (Isaiah 6:6–8) – the Old Testament is full of ex- amples. Jesus made the move with Zacchaeus (Luke

19:5), and with very many whom he helped. You could say how he found you, rather than the other way round.

4. *Justice.* This is a positive answer to the injustices mentioned earlier. Jesus cuts across human pride, as in the story he told of the Pharisee and the tax collector (Luke 18:9–14). Show how God is fair. Sin must be paid for (justice), but he allows his Son to take the punishment (grace). This may be a helpful way to speak about the cross. Other gods do as they please, not exercising justice.

5. *Action.* The actions of the Synoptic Gospels may work better than the words and arguments of John. The authority and love of Jesus are seen in his deeds.

A few practicalities

- *Friendship.* Many people give the impression of keeping their distance from members of other faiths, especially if they are of another colour. Open hostility is sometimes visible, but a covert separation is prevalent. A genuine interest (Key 2) is vital.

- *Attract rather than argue.* We are not aiming to show who is 'right', but to bring people to meet Jesus.

- *A quiet patience is needed.* We can show our faith as well as speak.

- *Respect.* Any putting down of another religion is unhelpful. Nor should we denigrate their holy books and writings, or condemn them for believing something different from us.

- It is worth remembering that many who claim to belong to other faiths are as 'nominal' in their beliefs as many who claim to be 'Christian' but only go to church at Christmas.

- *Best of all, pray and believe.* It may be a long journey, but Jesus is wanting to go with you to reach these 'other sheep who are not of this sheep pen'. He says, 'I must bring them also' (John 10:16).

The Stats

Here are the results of the survey on the 'family' section of 'Who I would like to help become a Christian'. I was very surprised so few mentioned their partners. Who would you have chosen? Fear not: I am going to treat each category as being very important and, hopefully, the relative you have in mind is included in one of the next nine chapters.

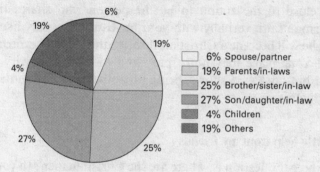

Chart 5: Who I would like to help become a Christian: family breakdown

6%

19%

19%

4%

27%

25%

- ☐ 6% Spouse/partner
- 19% Parents/in-laws
- 25% Brother/sister/in-law
- 27% Son/daughter/in-law
- 4% Children
- 19% Others

10 Husband

Here is the good news for every wife: God loves your husband even more than you do. Although you are giving all you've got for that man of yours, God has given his only Son to die for him. God wants your husband to become his son. I realise I am stating the obvious, but it is easy to forget this in our own concern. Relax in the love God feels for your husband (please include 'partner' in that term).

You do need to pay particular attention to Key 5. Indeed, you may not need to go beyond that. The question is: are you too close to the action to be the person who shares the Christian faith verbally with your husband? It is very likely that he will become a Christian through the help of someone else. Your place may be to pray and to trust. Passivity is hard but, as Key 5 shows, being proactive may be counter-productive.

A little help from my friends

The bigger question is: where are the Christian men? In your church, which men could – and should – be looking to share their faith with your husband and the other husbands of wives in a similar situation to you? Have any men in your church ever thought this through? Ask them! If that well-known glazed look appears, give them a few ideas. Refer them to the chapter on men in this book.

We had a brilliant minister in our church a few years ago. His system was simplicity itself. Every so often our car park would fall apart, with holes everywhere. Or the church interior would become quite scruffy, especially up towards the ceiling. The minister would pop round to the home of a lady member. Hubby would answer the door, see who it was, turn at once and call out, 'It's for you.' 'Hello, Bill!' the minister would say (after Bill had already called his wife). 'No – it's you I've come to see.' Shock, horror! 'Nothing to worry about! I've come looking for help. You know our car park. . . .'

A couple of Saturdays later would see Bill, sundry other 'outsider' husbands, the minister and some church men sorting out the car park. Quantities of doughnuts and coffee were consumed, a good time had by all, and relationships built. It was the same with redecorating the church or cleaning the graveyard: they all became a team, and the husbands were drawn in by the friendship and the sharing together.

You need to get your Christian men to help you. A 'curry and quiz' night, an evening ten-pin bowling, a full English breakfast with a good speaker: what are the men waiting for? Talk with your minister. Ask him to set the ball rolling. Suggest that he could plan some services with 'men on the outside' in mind.

What can *you* do?

As to what *you* can do, first of all accept that you have created a problem: you have dared to take the lead! You have made a major move in an important area of life: the spiritual. Your husband may, just may, be reacting to this by going the opposite way, and so re-establishing his 'headship' role. Be sure to check the chapter on men, as some of the characteristics of men mentioned there may belong to your husband.

The best thing you can do is simply be a Christian wife. Enjoy your marriage. Love your husband! Be the great partner and lover he wants, and that you truly can be. As the song said, 'accentuate the positive, eliminate the negative'. If you want to do specifically Christian things (for example, praying with the children), do them with his agreement, so you live at peace. Give the man your time, and don't be for ever rushing off to yet another church meeting. Don't be obvious in leaving a 'helpful Christian book' on his favourite easy chair!

• Finally, be ready to react in a loving way when spiritual matters are raised by him. You are not aiming to prove you are right, so let him take the lead. Jesus does not need defending. If the right moment comes (see Key 4), ask him simply if he would like to talk about the Christian faith – and accept his answer, one way or another.

Love, and patience – wouldn't you be a beautiful person with those two segments of the 'fruit of the Spirit' (Galatians 5:22–23)? I have seen very many husbands come to know Jesus Christ, and there is no reason why your man should not join their number.

11 Wife

If you are reading this book straight through from beginning to end, you will have seen the last chapter, so forgive some duplication! I have some good news for every husband: God loves your wife even more than you do, because his Son has died on the cross for her. God's longing is for your wife to be his daughter: relax in that fact. By the way, I include 'partner' when I speak of 'wife'.

The essentials

'Husbands, love your wives' (Ephesians 5:25). This is an excellent way to start sharing your faith with your wife. Be a brilliant husband. Tell your wife you love her, and show it by the things you do: the flowers you bring home, the help you give, the way you make love. Get the idea? Being a good husband is vital. Read the section on women a few pages back. She wants to see that Christianity is true. Are you a living witness by deed and word? You are the nearest example of a Christian she has: is she impressed? Perhaps best not to ask. . . .

Key 5 is vital here: you may well not be the person who helps your wife make the step to trust Christ. She is likely to come quietly on her own, or through the friendship and witness of another woman. Your place is to pray and to trust God to do his work. If you want to do specifically 'Christian' things at home, always talk them through first. For example, would your wife be happy for you to lead some simple family prayers with the children? Would it be possible to do this together? If you are going to chat about spiritual concerns, does your wife want to? If she does, then relax in the conversation, and don't let it drag on. If she does not, accept that fact with good grace.

Involving others

Part of being married is sharing friends, especially other couples. As you do this, make sure that your conversations are not such that a non-church or non-Christian partner is made to feel sidelined or excluded. Talk that is only about church and 'the Lord' can be very off-putting if you are not part of the set-up. Try not to be negative about your church or other Christians.

A word of serious caution: beware of appearing too friendly with other ladies at church. A jealous wife is the last thing you want. An unfaithful husband is the last thing she wants. If ever you find yourself saying to a Christian female friend, 'My wife doesn't understand me,' you are on the road to serious trouble. Here are some revolutionary questions. Do you go to too many Christian meetings? Is too much of your spare time taken up with 'church'? Do you get involved with other Christians too much? Balance is needed.

You do need help in sharing your faith with your wife. That is where the women in your church come in. They will be excellent at being friends, especially those living nearby. Encourage them to get to know your wife, doing the things women do so well together – talking, socialising, enjoying each other's company. Don't you wish you had their gifts? (I do!)

Talk with your minister and church leaders about putting on some good events especially for couples. For example, a meal (not necessarily on church premises), or evening events for ladies only, where someone could invite your wife and she would really *want* to go. What is your church doing?

Encourage your minister to put on an occasional service which would appeal to 'women on the outside', especially on Mother's Day, at Easter and at Christmas.

In the end it comes back to you. If you are a Christian husband who loves his wife, God can do the rest. Trust him and his timing. His love – even more than yours – will work the miracle.

12 Your Small Child

Would you like some good news? Parents who bring their children to Jesus Christ are encouraged and commended by him. 'Little children' are welcome, and we are all to 'receive the kingdom of God like a little child'. It says this in Mark 10:13–16 – an excellent starting place for learning about faith-sharing with your small child.

This chapter is specifically for parents. For advice on other children, see the earlier chapter which deals with them in general. I re-emphasise two points from it:

- Children can come to know Jesus at a young age. I personally look back to the age of seven when I first started out on my Christian life.
- If ever the word 'pressure' was anathema, it is here. As you faith-share with your small child, be very gentle. You are looking much more into the future than at the immediate present. 'The kingdom of God belongs to such as these' (Mark 10:14) means that they do not have to be forced in, but should be encouraged to stay there.

Getting going

It is never too soon to start to share your faith with your small child. It is amazingly precious for Dad to put his hands on Mum's tummy as the three of you pray together in the months before birth. Praying and singing with an unborn child is followed, quite naturally, with prayers and songs with the babe-in-arms.

In other words, let Jesus be a real member of the family from the beginning. If you become Christians when your children are small, simply start at that point and get going. If the children are big enough to understand, explain what has happened and agree a beginning. If you are praying together, remember that saying 'grace' at meals is a brief and encouraging reminder of our dependence on, and gratitude to, a loving Father.

Keeping going

Every family is unique. And almost every Christian family feels that other people's families get things much better spiritually than theirs does! Welcome to the club of parental failures – or so the devil would have you believe.

Never mind what the rest do; get a system you feel happy with and stick with it. It is bound to evolve as the children grow, and you will adapt in your faith-sharing according to age and circumstance. My wife and I would commend a few ideas:

- Try to find a small space each day to pray together as a family. Our time has usually been as breakfast is ending, with a few Bible verses and a simple offering of the day to God, as one person or another prays.
- There are some excellent Christian books for bedtime reading. As the television age marches on, parents who read to children are a disappearing breed and should be a protected species. Stories are great! I have read the entire Narnia series by C. S. Lewis to each of our four children, and the whole of *The Lord of the Rings* to two of them. There are great spiritual depths in these and other books.
- *The Lion Book of Children's Prayers* is brilliant for prayers with the individual child at bedtime. Don't rush this

special time. If your child is ill, pray with them very specifically, quietly laying hands on them if that seems appropriate. Jesus loves to heal children (see Mark 7:24–30).

- Be a family that enjoys being together. Talk about the things of God as naturally as you do about everything else. Children learn that Jesus can be part of *their* lives if he is part of *your* life.

- Make church-going a happy and expected Sunday activity. Encourage (rather than berate!) your church leaders to provide first-rate facilities for all ages of children, from a caring crèche upwards. It is through the activities and teachings of the children's groups that your child will discover the value of a personal faith which is independent of yours.

- Visits to all-age events such as Spring Harvest, New Wine, Easter People, and church-away weekends will help your children to hear of how a faith can be theirs.

Just once more . . .

Take it easy! You are likely to be a major means of helping your child to faith, but another may help them to come to that personal relationship with Jesus. So relax, be happy, and enjoy sharing Jesus together as a young family. It may ease you into the next chapter, too!

13 Your Older Child

Welcome to the chapter where two words come into their own: negotiation and patience. The art of the first and the gift of the second will be vital. Let me explain.

Negotiation

I am not going to put a lower age limit on 'older' because for one it will be eight or nine, for another 13. There is no upper limit, because your child is always your child, and will behave as such in certain circumstances (for example when your married son/daughter phones to ask how you make custard). But the time will come when a child cannot simply be told what to do, and explanations will be needed. This is especially so in faith-sharing. 'Why should I?' is a fair question. Everything that follows in this chapter is on the basis of talking, give-and-take and (here is a word Christians struggle with) compromise.

If you have become Christians while your children have been growing, or if you have not been living the Christian life as you would have wished and now want things to change, a family get-together, or a series of one-to-one chats, may nip a lot of problems in the bud. Honesty over perceived failures on your part will go down well, as will genuine requests for reasonable help. Explain why you feel a particular course of action would be better. The sooner children become part of working out how the whole family should function as a Christian family, the easier it will be for you to share your faith with your older children.

You may experience a strong reaction against your new faith, especially from much older children. One of my friends wrote to each of his children to explain his new-found faith, only to find that they thought he had 'lost it' completely as they expressed concerns about his mental state.

Patience

Instant, overnight conversions do happen – but rarely. St Monica is famous for one thing. For 34 years she prayed for her profligate son to become a Christian. She shed many tears. Only after all that time did her son turn to Christ. His name? St Augustine, arguably the most influential Christian thinker outside of the Bible. You will need to 'keep on keeping on' praying and trusting for your older child.

Accept your limitations

You will know these already, but I set them out so you realise you are normal!

- It would be wholly exceptional if you did very much overt faith-sharing. Too much talking may come across as laying down the law and be counterproductive.
- Realise the huge external pressure your child is under from the world system, education, aggressive advertising and peer pressure.
- Try to understand the almost impossible internal family tension. Your child is trying to become independent as adulthood approaches, which means growing away from you. And yet you want them to hold on to your faith?
- As part of this, you can only suggest a course of action in the spiritual areas of life. Having said that, it is *your* home

the child will leave. Therefore you must retain the Christian spirit of the home, with necessary careful explanations.

- Your child's culture is very different from yours in a rapidly changing world: be sure to look back to the chapters on teenagers and generation X.

Some positives

All is not doom and gloom! I have enjoyed the Christian love of older children as a tremendous boost to my own life. What can be done?

- Agree to be a family together at least on special occasions, such as all being in church on Mother's Day and Christmas Day. Consider saying grace at mealtimes.
- For the older child still at home, get your church to have irresistibly good youth groups for sub-teens, younger teens, older teens and twenties. Is this an absolute priority in your church, with excellent leaders and wonderful activities?
- A 'gap' year may be a real step forward. Drop in a suggestion, and encourage any moves by your child. They will depend on God in a Third World situation, whether they plan to or not.
- Be ready always for crisis situations. Digging your child out of a hole, especially non-judgementally, will be a brilliant piece of faith-sharing. Never shirk from saying, 'I'll be praying for you,' when the phone call comes at 3 a.m., or on the morning of the exam, or before the interview.
- Best of all, whatever happens, give your positive, for ever love. A final word to dads – I find an occasional big hug is a great way of faith-sharing, as well as love-giving!

14 Father

It can be hard sharing your faith with members of your family, and none more so than with 'Dad'. The problem is stated very simply: he has always seen his rôle as telling you what to do and how to live – and now *you* want to give *him* some advice? Tread carefully.

Your success in faith-sharing will depend a great deal on your relationship. Have you got any relationship at all? If so, is it good? Your first task is to build a really good rapport between you and your dad. As you have grown, he will almost certainly have felt distanced from you. You are not the little one who used to sit on his knee and delight in his off-key nursery rhymes! It is hard to be a dad (believe me), and he feels a failure quite often, although he cannot tell anyone (again, believe me – and now my secret is out!). Your helping him to know your love, and affirming him, will be a major part of faith-sharing.

Dad may wonder at your Christian faith. He may criticise it openly. But – and it is a big but – he wants to be proud of you. If, therefore, your Christian life goes well, he will react positively. He will be pleased your life is good, that your Christian marriage is a happy one, that you can face adversity with courage. All these are gifts from God, and they are real ways of faith-sharing with him.

If you are at home, work hard at showing your dad respect. 'Honour' is God's word in the Ten Commandments (Exodus 20:12) and it does not mean you have to agree with him always! Negotiate, especially about specifically Christian matters. If you need to do something, find a *good* moment to explain. This will be particularly necessary when you need his financial help (as when your youth group is off to Soul Survivor or New Wine and you need the cash). Whatever you do, never use God as an excuse (check out Mark 7:9–13).

A few ideas

- Dad will ask questions and make comments from time to time. Ride the punches! Smile rather than frown. Remember, 'a gentle answer turns away wrath' (Proverbs 15:1). Get the idea? His very aggression is a defence mechanism. Explain your position kindly, giving some positives for your beliefs.
- You are more likely to take this reactive stance, but there will be an occasional opportunity to say something without your dad taking the lead. If you have had a particular blessing, or you have known God do a special thing, and you can share it naturally and spontaneously, then go for it – in words he can understand.
- If he is elderly (or even if he's not!), why not take him out? Check out the chapter on older people. It might open up opportunities for conversation.
- Invite your dad (and mum of course!) to stay. If he is a widower, or divorced, this would be excellent, and he could share naturally in your Christian home. If you have 'family prayers', invite him to be there, with the option of declining.
- Does he enjoy music and videos and books? Older dads may, and there are some excellent Christian publications he might enjoy.
- Check out the chapter on men. What is your dad's local church doing? What are his Christian neighbours doing?

And finally – love the old boy to bits! Dads are sometimes not easily loved. You may be able to share your faith through your love better than your words.

15 Mother

'Good ol' Mum!' 'Mother knows best!' 'Who decides? Mother decides.' 'The best mum in the world.'

The things we say about our mothers. There they are, on pedestals built by us, their adoring children. Unfortunately, these expressions of appreciation militate against faith-sharing. If Mother can do no wrong, how can she need a Saviour? If she knows best, how do you have something better? Don't worry, this is not an insurmountable problem, and the news about faith-sharing with your mum is almost all good and positive.

Mother's little helper

That's you! As a starter in faith-sharing with her, be that 'little helper'. Even in days of so-called 'equality' and 'enlightenment', mothers carry big burdens at home, and your help in practical ways will say a great deal about your Christianity. After you have left home, an occasional visit which includes doing a much-needed spot of gardening, or painting the bathroom, will be a great move.

Most mums love their children and want to see them do well. If you live a normal, happy Christian life she will be very pleased. If you can avoid going to great extremes, so much the better. Your mum will be delighted that her grandchildren are being brought up in a loving Christian environment. The way you live will speak volumes about your faith.

It is only natural if your mum wants to understand what is going on in your life, and that includes your life of faith.

Mums are much better than dads at sitting down and chatting. So you can be much more proactive, sharing your faith in a natural, easy-going way, while at all costs avoiding 'preaching'. Give her the opportunity to ask questions and to express reservations. Mum is also more likely to start a conversation, and to ask what goes on at your church, youth group, school CU and so on. Give happy and positive answers.

Mums also enjoy going out. What does she enjoy? Is there a good event you could go to together? Does she enjoy music? There is a vast range of Christian music to appeal to most tastes. She may enjoy reading: have you got a good book which you have enjoyed? One which is not 'over the top' would be best!

The usual question arises: what are the women in your church doing for the ladies of their district? Can you take your mum to a service where she would not feel out of place?

What I am trying to say is, you can be quite positive as you share your faith with your mother. If she puts up the shutters, accept that with good grace. But a mum is one of the happier members of the family when it comes to faith-sharing.

A cautionary tale

The picture is not always rosy. My grandmother had the singular distinction of coming through the Welsh revival without being affected by it: quite an achievement! My mother was the most beautiful and gentle Christian, but she was four years into her marriage when that Christian life started. For 21 years she lovingly showed her Christian faith to her own mother. When we moved to another town, my mother would write graciously to Gran every week. And every week a letter critical of my mother's faith would come back. I saw my mother in tears over those letters. Yet she never ceased to love her mother, and to pray for her.

After those 21 years, my mother died, aged 45. It was only six months later that Gran trusted Christ – six months before she herself died. Her words were, 'I want to follow Joan's way' – the way of my mother, Joan, was the way of Jesus. Take heart: the road may be long, but God's love for your mum means that he will keep searching until he finds her.

16 Brothers and Sisters

Brothers and sisters come in two sizes – younger and older! To help you with both, this chapter is in two halves. Let's look at the younger variety first.

Younger brothers and sisters

For this part, you need to have a younger brother or sister, probably no older than ten or so. If you love Jesus, how can you share that with a younger child in your family? Here are two suggestions and a few ideas.

Be a friend

You may not have realised this, but your young brother/sister looks up to you. You are a sort of role model: in other words, they would like to be like you. You are their hero! Of course, if you are horrid, you will be their enemy. So be kind, and positive, to them. Share your life with them in a natural way.

Be a sort of best friend. I know they are little, and like 'baby' things compared with you. But they will really value your fun, your help and the time you spend with them. You can enjoy playing together, and also helping with the tough job of starting to learn how to do things.

If you are a friend like this, they will see how wonderful it is to know Jesus. You don't have to be perfect and, if you have to say 'sorry' sometimes, don't be too proud to apologise. As you share your faith by the way you live, there will be good opportunities to talk as well. You have more chance than your parents. Make sure you are gentle. I hope no one forced you to trust Jesus, so lay off the pressure. But, if you talk about everything else, why not talk about Jesus sometimes?

Be an includer

It is tough on a big brother or sister, having to include 'junior', but you can do it! Don't make your younger brother or sister feel pushed out. They don't have to be around *all* the time. If you involve them in your church's activities for young people, and they have groups for different ages, your brother/sister will really value their own group. The attitude of you and your friends as Christians will either show the love of Jesus or make them feel pushed out – which do you want?

Be enthusiastic about the Christian music you enjoy and the events you go to. Do you go to a Christian camp, house party, Easter or summer event, or anything like that? You know how good it is for you and, if you share it, it could be great for your brother/sister as well. They may meet Jesus there. How brilliant to go through your life with a brother or sister who is a real Christian!

My story

I'm the eldest in my family. The very first person I remember telling about Jesus was my sister, who is seven years younger than me. She says that it was I who told her about Jesus, and that is how she became a Christian. I was not even a teenager at the time. She's still a Christian today, so it can be done!

Now we switch to brothers and sisters of the older variety!

Older brothers and sisters

Here, we will look at all siblings not mentioned under the first heading – so it covers a multitude of different sorts of people! I include teenagers upwards, and brothers- and sisters-in-law as well.

Getting to know you

With quite a number of these, the first question must be: how well do you know them? Even if you have grown up with them, they will have changed drastically since they were small children, so Key 2 needs revisiting. It may also be helpful to check the chapters on teenagers and generation X. A further question is: how close are you to them in age? Some people say that a generation gap can be as small as three to five years, so there may have to be some cross-generational understanding.

Having done a little background thinking, the next step is to do some 'getting to know you'. Before any faith-sharing, there needs to be a build-up of friendship. If there is a good relationship, you may find yourself the confidante. This is a tough old world, and a hand of love genuinely held out may be taken with gratitude. Work on the relationship, not just for the opportunities but for the mutual sharing of friendship and love.

If you are at home together, be an ally. If you are close in age, share interests, including going out to events together, especially of a social nature. You will have things going on where you would like them to join you: the *quid pro quo* is your going with them to what they enjoy. Both of you can say 'no thanks' without rancour, and your faith should be strong enough to enable you to go to most places without compromise.

At a distance

Inevitably, many of the people in this category will be at some distance from you geographically, as they, or you, go to university, get a house, get married, find a job elsewhere, and so on. The amazing advances in communication should ease this problem. My sons email each other from different parts of the country frequently. Their mobile phones mean they can chat from the top of a bus or in the bath. Time can be made to pop over to wherever in the car. Any relationship, to be meaningful, must be worked on.

If you are at a distance, you may be in a reactive situation in speaking of your faith. As crises arise, don't be afraid to say that you are praying for them. A simple card offering support ('I'll be praying – call me if you need me') may be good. If you are thinking about brothers- and sisters-in-law, it may be worth treating them more as friends, and looking at those chapters later in this book. It may take the pressure off by ignoring family ties.

However, with your generational closeness and your family links, you could be an ideal person to share your faith with an older brother or sister. Unlike parents, who have to tread softly, your faith-sharing could come naturally. Indeed, it may well be expected, and there might be a sense of disappointment if you never did say anything. Be ready for disagreement and debate, and don't let them get to you. But you could be the means of helping a brother or sister (and in-law) to meet Christ. You will need to know your stuff (Key 1), and when it is a good time to talk (Key 4). In some chapters I have advised extreme caution. With your older brothers and sisters I'd say think positively. If you have a good, close relationship, look out for real faith-sharing opportunities that arise naturally, and go for it.

17 Grandparents

Whoever you are, whatever age you are, this could be a great chapter for your faith-sharing. If you are wondering who on earth you could share your faith with, think of 'Grandpa' and 'Gran'.

Wonderful you

Grandparents are brilliant. A large part of the reason for this is that they think you are so special. You have no idea how excited they were about your birth. You have elevated their very status. 'We are a grandmother' was one of the most famous things Margaret Thatcher ever said. You are one of the most favourite people in their lives. They may love you even more (don't tell this to anyone) than your parents. They are willing to forgive almost anything you do wrong and will indulge you and spoil you rotten. It's tough being a grandchild, but you can do it.

What you need to do is build on this popularity. If you were to phone, that would be welcome. If you visit, they will really enjoy your company, your stories, and especially your time and love. Whatever your age, and whatever their age, you can have an amazing bond of love and togetherness and a unique rapport.

Conversely, when you have your own home, invite them over. If they are unable to travel because of mobility problems or lack of transport, go and get them. They will enjoy your simple family prayers and coming to church with you.

Faith-sharing in the context of your family life will be natural and genuine.

Wonderful them

Yes, indeed, grandparents are great. You have a huge advantage when it comes to sharing your faith with them: they are almost certain to have a background of knowledge of Christianity, however long ago it was. Many of their generation went to church or Sunday school, and a look back at the chapter on older people will help you here. Even now your grandparents may have a real interest in spiritual things and enjoy programmes like *Songs of Praise*.

Church is not an alien place, either. If you stay with them, or they with you, include a Sunday service. They will enjoy a traditional style. However, they might also appreciate a newer type of service if you explain what is going on, and if it is both 'real' and friendly. This is an excellent way to share your faith, and a chat over lunch afterwards may be very fruitful.

The grandparental age group has time to enjoy reading and listening to music. Think of good books and CDs as gifts. But it is *you* who are the key. Grandparents do have time to read and listen, but they would rather talk. Sit down and chat. They want to hear about your life.

Enthuse about what you do. Your faith should fit into this quite naturally. They will hear it from you better than almost anyone else. You could be the ideal person to talk with them about Jesus, his love for them and his longing that they should know him in their older days. Love them to bits! Encourage them to be ready for heaven.

Should you share your faith with your grandparents? Yes. Do it with huge love and care, but do it. You could be the one who helps them – more than anyone else.

18　In-laws and Out-laws

The out-laws

The title of this chapter needs a little explanation. We will look here at the specific categories of father- and mother-in-law, as brothers- and sisters-in-law have been covered under 'Older Brothers and Sisters'. But I want to say a brief word about all our other relatives – the 'out-laws': uncles, aunts, cousins and so on. When it comes to more distant relations, my advice is: treat them as 'other friends' and go on to that chapter, where I have included them. Your family ties may, or may not, help; they are, at least, an excuse to keep in touch.

If they are older, such as elderly uncles and aunts, I would put them in a similar category to grandparents, so go back to the last chapter. If they are of a similar age to you, such as cousins, the chapters on brothers and sisters will apply.

The in-laws

Now, look, they can't be all that bad: after all, they produced your partner! A lovely lady cannot suddenly become a dragon just because you got married and she therefore acquired the title 'mother-in-law'! What *is* your relationship with your in-laws? It could – and should – be good. To a large extent it is up to you. If you are kind and loving, there is no reason why it should be otherwise.

If you are to build a relationship in which you can share your faith, it will take time. Visits to the in-laws are vital.

They will really appreciate the time you give and the interest you show. In a world where people seem to have little time for each other, the very unexpectedness of your involvement will prove a great plus. The in-laws have a genuine interest in you and your partner and would love to be included in what you are doing. You will often be a topic of conversation, which (whatever you think) is likely to be positive and concerned.

Invite them over to your home, too. If that means proverbially biting the bullet, still do it. If they live nearby, let them pop round. When that becomes a burden, talk through with your spouse, and with them if you can, what would be a happier number of visits. If they live at a distance, let them come and stay for a few days. Include them in your family prayers at breakfast. Take them to your church. Be natural, and be yourselves as Christians. You may find the chapters 'Father' and 'Mother' helpful here.

Your children will be a real asset in your faith-sharing, especially when they are small. Grandparents will want to take a turn at putting junior to bed, with the routine including a 'Bible' story and a prayer. The in-laws will want to fit in with the norm.

When it comes to the question of speaking directly about your faith, you may find, to your surprise, that you are a good person to share your faith with an in-law. You may have a far better chance than your partner. You are just that one step further away from the action, and you do not have the build-up of past problems. Opposite-sex relationships may be of particular value here. My dad is a Christian, but I reckon his relationship with my wife is better than his relationship with me, and she can chat about all sorts of things with him, for which I am grateful. Similarly, I get on well with my mother-in-law.

Of course, the suggestions in Key 4, about knowing the right time to speak, apply here. But do be positive. Love your in-laws, and encourage them to know Jesus.

A good story

For whom did Jesus perform one of his first miracles? Answer: a mother-in-law! The cameo incident in Mark 1:29–31 should encourage every one of us who has an in-law. Jesus brought blessing to Simon Peter's house by healing his mother-in-law. What a blessing it would be if your in-laws were to let Jesus touch their lives. He can. He will. Trust him.

19   Best Friend

Let me set the scene: you are a Christian and your very best friend is not. It may be that you have recently trusted Christ or, having been a Christian for some time, a good friendship has developed with a non-Christian. What should you do? Answer: be the very best friend you could be! Well done for having a close friend who does not yet know Jesus Christ: far too many Christians have hardly any non-Christian friends at all. As a Christian, be an even better friend, because Jesus wants to be their best friend, too.

Be positive

Friendship is all about sharing. If you want to share your faith, you must share your friend's interests too. Just because you are a Christian doesn't mean you will switch off to everything other than 'church' and 'God'. If you get into 'non-Christian' activities, draw any line as graciously as possible. Be positive, even when having to be negative. What do I mean? Let me give you an example. When your friend suddenly explodes with, 'Oh, God!' your reply is, 'Now you're coming along – praying out loud!' Say it with a grin!

I'm sure you won't, but don't push your faith down their throat. A close friendship means talking about anything and everything. The expression 'gossip the gospel' is good here. You are bound to talk about your faith at some point. Be natural. Talk about spiritual things as you do about everything else, as and when the subject comes up in conversation. Humour and honesty will work wonders. When you are asked, 'What did you do on Sunday?' answer with enthusiasm. Tell your friend what they missed!

Welcome along

Look out for opportunities to involve your best friend in what you do. If you have enjoyed a Christian CD, lend it to them. If you are going to New Wine, or Spring Harvest, or Easter People (or something similar), why not invite them along with you? If your church has a good barbecue planned, or even a holiday, would your friend like to tag along?

Best of all, look out for positive ways of helping your friend meet Jesus. We looked at Philip and Nathaniel in Key 1. But it is worth looking closely at the incident again in John 1:43–51, because it shows how a genuine, enthusiastic and non-pushy invitation helped a best friend become a real disciple of Jesus Christ. Philip did not pretend he knew all the answers, but his friendship got through the defensive question and won the day.

Of course, Nathaniel could have said 'no'. Your best friend may say that as well. If they do, accept their answer with good grace and retain their friendship. However, there is a cautionary note. I once had a best friend who decided he would walk away from God. I gave him my very best shot, but we drifted apart. God asks the question, 'Do two walk together unless they have agreed to do so?' (Amos 3:3). I am sorry that part of the cost of being a Christian may occasionally mean losing a good friend who is not going to be a Christian. If the friendship does end, be sure it's not because of *you*, and always keep the door open.

Let me end this chapter positively with two thoughts:

• Your close friendship may be the very best means by which your friend can meet Jesus. Pray for right moments, right words and a positive response.

- God loves your best friend very much and he will reach them one way or another. Although the friend I mentioned has not been in touch for many years, I still pray for him regularly. God's love goes on, and so can ours.

20 Boy/Girlfriend

This may be a tricky chapter for you (though not as tough as the next one!) if you are wanting to share your faith with your romantically attached friend.

Hot questions

- If you are going out with someone who is not a Christian, are you able to bring your faith into your relationship? Is your faith part of your relationship? Wherever you go, whoever you are with, you can't leave Jesus behind.
- Do you want a long-term romantic relationship with a non-Christian? Where will it take you?
- Are you kidding yourself that you are 'going out for evangelistic purposes'? I must confess I did that in my teens. It rarely works and is no basis for a romance. If your partner tumbles to what you are doing, what will they think? At the very least your motives will be misconstrued.

Positive suggestions

It may be that you have recently become a Christian, and you really are in love with that person. What should you do?

- Be a great friend. Don't drop them like a hot potato.
- Be good. You know what I mean.
- Don't be for ever preaching. Share your faith naturally, when the opportunity comes.

- Do things together. Go to church and your age group activity.
- You may be very pleasantly surprised at how they would enjoy one of the excellent Christian holiday/conferences such as Spring Harvest, New Wine, Easter People and others that are equally as good, and you can have fun being there together.
- Do you listen to music together? Christian music is pretty good these days, and most secular styles can be found in the Christian music scene.
- Why not go for it? Share your faith with enthusiasm, honesty and humour. Be positive and happy – and wait for the reaction! If they love you, they may be drawn by that love towards the love God has for them.

Will it work?

Well, you know them better than most people. Key 2 should have been easy. You will have to accept that your faith-sharing may not work, and you cannot force them to agree.

You may not be the one who helps your boy/girlfriend become a Christian. If it causes a parting of the ways, do not leave them unkindly or in a 'holier-than-thou' manner. The last thing you want is their blaming God for your method of ending the relationship.

On the other hand, I did once go out with a girl who was not a Christian. We went to hear an evangelist, and she gave her life to Christ. We went out for a long time after that. Even though the romance eventually ended for other reasons, we are both still keen Christians today (and happily married to other people!). I *did* help her meet Jesus. This is not a negative chapter. But if things are very serious between you, you will want to check out the next chapter as well.

21 Fiancé(e)

Here you are, engaged to be married to someone who is not a Christian. (If your spouse-to-be *is* a Christian, you are in the wrong chapter: go on to number 26.) How have you got to this situation? Either you got engaged knowing you were a Christian and your intended was not, or you have become a Christian since your engagement.

This book is not about marriage guidance, but about faith-sharing. Let's be positive again. You may want to read the previous chapter as well.

What to do

Can I assume something? You do love this fiancé(e) of yours, don't you? OK. Love them even more! What kind of faith-sharing gives the impression that Jesus makes us love people *less*? I'm not implying that you should go further physically: presumably you are living within the Bible's guidelines here. But being engaged is a commitment to one person, so all your love should be theirs.

In other chapters, I have advised caution in saying anything. Here the reverse is the case. Subject only to finding the right time (Key 4), you are going to have to talk things through. If your faith in Jesus Christ matters you will want to share it with your fiancé(e). Whatever matters to you should be important to them, and vice versa. This faith is crucial to your life and the very motivation for all you are and do. They will need to be keenly aware of what that means to you and the way you think and act. It will impinge on every aspect of your marriage. Does your spouse-to-be want that?

You need to be honest. Every couple has to work out how they will face life together. Is your faith a problem or an opportunity? Emphasise the positive aspects of what God has done (and is doing) for you, and what he can do for you both in your relationship and your marriage. If you have read the chapters 'Husband' and 'Wife', disregard everything they say about backing off. Now is the time, during your engagement, to talk things through. Just because you are a Christian and your fiancé(e) is not, it would not be good to break the relationship until you were satisfied that all your conversations about your faith had proved negative. But you will need to make some decisions.

What to decide

You, in your own mind, without necessarily telling your fiancé(e), will need to make a personal decision about your marriage. You are at a crunch time in your life. You must know, deep down, whatever you say to anyone else, that you are entering unknown territory as you get married. Marriage generally is under serious threat: one in two end in divorce. We are agreed that a divorce is not in your planning. God says specifically: 'Don't be yoked together with unbelievers' (2 Corinthians 6:14). A 'yoke' only joins two together.

You will know of people in your church who have non-Christian spouses, and the difficulties they encounter. Marriage is about being at one. That is why a good question to ask is: 'Do two walk together unless they have agreed to do so?' (Amos 3:3). Future walking together depends on doing that now. Do *not* be kidded by promises like 'I will change', or 'You can be a Christian/go to church/ live your life – I won't stop you or get in the way'. They mean 'You go your way, I'll go mine', which is not 'two walking together'.

It is possible that your fiancé(e) will come to church with you during your engagement. Be brutally honest: is it to please you and be with you, or is it out of a genuine spiritual interest? Are they really 'tuning in'? You will need a scrupulous kind of honesty which you will find difficult to have in your far-from-objective position. But you must do it. I do apologise for coming across so strongly, but it is better to face the tough truth now than be sorry later.

If your fiancé(e) is to be your life-long partner, they really do need to know Jesus. Never threaten or bribe. But do be realistic. Share your faith with loving enthusiasm, encouraging a joint commitment to God as well as to each other. Marriage is meant to be his gift (Genesis 2:24). Enjoy it with him! That is why, of every situation in this book, yours may be the most critical, because your faith-sharing could have the longest lasting consequences for you.

Remember: God loves you and your fiancé(e). He has your best interests at heart. Share your faith with love and concern, honestly and openly. Leave the outcome to your heavenly Father.

22 Schoolfriend

Some of the closest friendships you will ever share are while you are at school, so enjoy them! How can you share your faith with your friends at school?

Be a good friend!

At least one of those friends may be your best friend (in which case look back to that chapter). Whether or not a particular person is your 'best friend', be a good friend to them. Good friends are few and far between. Be loyal. The fact that you do not gossip, or talk about them behind their back, will be a real sign of your Christian life. How you act is going to be at least as important as anything you say.

You can share your faith quite naturally by being positive and being fun. Do normal things together. Friends talk. They help each other with homework. They laugh. They listen to music. Why shouldn't you do these things as a Christian? That does not stop you having God's standards for your life. Your friend will respect what you do, especially if you can explain that your actions come from your faith. Stick to what you believe, and don't make a big deal of it. It is not just Christians who don't smoke, who drink 'lemonade on the rocks', who avoid drugs and don't go 'all the way' with sex. It is how you do these things that counts. God is no spoilsport, and your happy Christian lifestyle will say a lot without your speaking a word.

Be around

Friends are for good times, to share fun and laughter. Even more, friends are for the tough times. While you are at school some of your friends will face hard situations. Be ready to share your faith by the way you act when they arise. Here are a few possibilities:

- *Problems at home.* Your friend may well have an unhappy home life. In your class there will be children from broken homes, single-parent families and divorcing parents. Your friends will be badly hurt. One of my sons sat with a friend late one night talking through the pain of his friend discovering his parents were separating. (If he had phoned me to say why he was out so late it might have helped – but that's another story!) Your Christian concern will be really valuable.
- *Failure.* Not passing an exam, not making the team, losing a boy/girlfriend: life can be cruel. An arm round the shoulder works wonders!
- *Bad behaviour.* You can support a friend even when they get it wrong. Another of my sons got it right when he brought his very drunk friend home for the night and we looked after him. His parents knew he was with us, but on a 'need to know basis' they did not find out about his state. He learned his lesson, gave my wife some flowers and saw my son's faith in action.
- *Bereavement.* When someone special to your friend dies, it is an important thing to be around, helping them through.

You get the idea? Be there, and your faith will shine through quite naturally.

Saying it how it is

In many of the situations mentioned, a quiet word will be appreciated, such as, 'I'll be praying for you.' Your friend would be glad to know that. Something gentle and positive is going to be much better than going on about what they do wrong. If your friend swears, what did you expect? Don't let it get to you. Simply because you are known to be a Christian they may ease back on some of their non-Christian behaviour.

You need to be happily open about your faith. Don't be ashamed to admit to knowing Jesus Christ. You won't have to make a big thing about it: as soon as anyone knows, the news will get round. Invite your close friends to anything good you've got happening in or through your church or its youth organisations (you will have to go to *their* events, too, as long as you and your parents agree with what will go on).

Does your school have a Christian Union? Check out that chapter later on in the book. Don't panic if your friends will not join you there, but it will say a lot to them if you go.

Go for it

The good news is, very many people become Christians while they are at school. Your friends are growing into independent adults. Part of that is growing away from their parents. If their parents are not Christians, that independence can include discovering a faith of their own. You can help them to meet Jesus.

Pray for a good opportunity to speak of your faith (Key 4). Find a good place for a chat (Key 6): is there a room in your home you could use? Ask if your friend would like to hear about your faith and what God means to you. Take it from there. Look again at Key 7: wouldn't it be amazing to help a friend become a Christian? Then you could go on together (Key 8). Trust God – you are one of his representatives in your school!

23 Friend at University/College

If you are a student at a university or college, you have an excellent opportunity to share your faith with your fellow students. Here are a few thoughts and ideas to help you.

Being around

What a great time to be a friend! Beware of the Christian trap of having only Christian friends while at university, and of only going to lectures and the Christian Union. Get stuck in to the activities of your hall, your digs or your houseful of students, and share in the fun. There are many non-Christians who will appreciate and value your friendship as university can be a lonely place.

In days gone by (I speak from personal experience), Christians were hardly seen around the Student Union, and rarely got involved in student activities. The mere presence of a Christian is a key element in faith-sharing. As you do this, your good, positive standards will not be frowned on, especially if you don't come across as 'negative'. As you live closely alongside other students, they will be aware of your faith and will be watching you. You don't have to be ultra-perfect, but it will be novel for many students to have a real Christian around. The vast majority will have had little or no contact with Christianity, so your life is faith-sharing.

Opportunities to share

University is a place where a lot of thinking goes on. It is a place where futures are planned and new beginnings made.

It is a time to give God a chance. Those who have never had a thought for spiritual concerns may use this opportunity to work things out. It will not be impossible for you to share your faith with people who are doing well and yet realise there is an extra dimension which they wish to explore.

You may want to look back at the previous chapter ('Schoolfriend') to see the section 'Be around'. When at university, a student is faced with a variety of situations where your Christian friendship will come into play. Courses and exams bring real pressures. Loneliness and depression are frequent problems. Home life may be missed very badly. Family relationships can fall apart, and romances come and go with painful consequences for some. Yours may be the shoulder to cry on, and your prayers will be very much appreciated at crisis moments. Never be afraid to offer God's love and care in what you say, as well as how you act. By being supportive, and speaking of how God has helped or is helping you, you will be able to share your faith as maybe no one else can.

University gives great opportunities to talk about, discuss and debate major issues. Your aim is neither to argue nor to prove you are right. God does not need defending! Key 1 is crucial here. Know what you are talking about, and share happily that the Christian faith is true and is real in your own life and personal experience. Remember, several people talking together is different from one-to-one: an individual may want to chat quietly later and be much more sympathetic. It is in the more private chats that progress can be made towards the discovery of a personal faith.

Teamwork

With your fellow Christian students, much can be accomplished in faith-sharing. A Christian Union can put on excellent events for outsiders, with good bands, speakers and lively discussions. Even nearer to your friends, your hall or house could have its own cell group, open to everyone. Half a dozen sitting round one evening a week may give key openings for faith-sharing, but don't make it look like gang warfare on an unfortunate visitor!

Somewhere nearby should be a lively church which may well be welcoming to students. Involve them, as well as the university chaplaincy, in your faith-sharing activities. Together with your Christian friends, much can be done. A university evangelistic mission often helps students come to faith.

Large numbers of Christians look back to their years at university as a time when their faith either started or really took off. As a Christian student, God has given you a door of opportunity to share your faith. Be sure to walk through!

24 Other Friends

This is in some ways a 'sweep up' chapter – anyone not mentioned elsewhere fits in here, as it were! But it is important because 'friends' can include all sorts of people, from more distant relatives to a neighbour who is more than just someone down the road. How can we share our faith with our friends?

Be a friend

It sounds obvious, but life can be too busy to have friends if we are not careful. 'Being a friend' means doing something positive. It means making time, being available for friendship. Even at church, folk can be no more than nodding acquaintances. How well do you know the person with whom you would be friends? This applies to relatives who are not immediate, such as uncles and aunts and cousins. Revisiting Key 2 would help. It is amazing how long a time can pass between meetings. Family get-togethers may only happen at weddings and funerals, or the Christmas reunion, when there are so many present that each one only gets a couple of minutes.

I find I have to make a special effort to see one or two of my cousins, and occasionally 'do lunch' or arrange a get-together over a coffee. Otherwise it could be literally years before we, as distant relatives, meet up. My memory is so poor, I have a phone list of those I need to call, updating it every few months. I include both far-away friends and relatives on this.

By doing this, I try to be aware of their joys and sorrows, hopes and needs. As a friend I must be aware as well as be available. It must be known that we care, and this concern has to be expressed or it can be forgotten. It also means fitting in, as well as expecting the other person to fit in with us. If we are to expect a friend, or more distant relative, to hear what we have to say, they may have to share their current story first. We will have to go to them if we want them to come our way.

Share naturally

Part of the secret of faith-sharing here is simply to live the Christian life in a natural, normal way. Enjoy life! Not everyone does. The impact of this lifestyle can be very great. The way you face the pressures and pains of life with God's help, and come through, will speak volumes. When the openings come, share your faith quite naturally, speaking of it as you do about everything else.

Take opportunities as they arise. This will be especially so when your friend or relative is going through times of sorrow or need, and also on occasions of particular happiness. If something wonderful has happened in your immediate past where God has really blessed you, don't save it only for your Christian friends. Tell the world! A couple of months before writing this, God did a wonderful thing in my own personal life. It was so good I told almost everyone I met! This included several non-Christian friends and relatives. Every last one of them was clearly happy for me and delighted I had told them. It was open and positive faith-sharing.

What I found, once again, was that I had no need to be 'pushy'. I simply answered their question 'How are you?' with, 'I've had the most amazing thing happen,' and took it from there. It not only enabled me to speak of God's love, but brought me much closer to these friends and relatives and encouraged further meetings and talks together. Part of the secret was talking about what God had done through Jesus. So easily we chicken out by speaking of our church but not of our Lord. My recent conversations have shown me that people are much more interested in Jesus.

It may not be something God has done so much as something he has shown you – perhaps through a book you are reading. Books can present amazing and natural opportunities to enthuse about God. I have learned now to let the Holy Spirit give me the nudge to be bold in what I say. We have something – *someone* – worth sharing with our friends and relatives. If it were anything else, we would speak of it – so why not speak of Jesus and what he is doing for us? I'm certainly going to share my faith more readily with this lesser-known group from now on. Why don't you give it a go too?

25 Another Christian

The survey about faith-sharing brought one particularly unexpected reply: 'I would like to share my faith with the vicar'! It certainly set me thinking that I ought to include one chapter on faith-sharing with the Christians we know. (If your fellow Christian has drifted or moved deliberately from their faith, go on to the next chapter.)

Christians together

One of the dangers of being close to other Christians is taking our mutual faith for granted. We assume all to be well, rarely being concerned about the spiritual dimension of their lives. This can be so with those at our church, other leaders, and even with our family and those we love – partners, parents and children.

Part of the secret of faith-sharing and encouragement with another Christian is to be together. I don't mean at church, where we meet in larger numbers. We need time one-to-one, or in a foursome. We can chat over a cuppa or a meal – at home or out – or go out for the evening or shopping. Why not go to a Christian festival with a Christian friend or relative? There are so many, especially at Easter and in the summer.

If we are not careful, we take our Christian friends and relatives for granted, especially in this spiritual sphere. Our conversations, at best, are about what goes on at church. Leaders take up their time with 'who's doing what next Sunday'. There is little personal sharing of our faith.

Let's talk

Even with another Christian, Key 4 (finding the right time) is important. However, there must be times when we can at least say, 'I'm praying for you.' I love someone telling me that! A word of encouragement works wonders, too. In a busy church, a minister has too many people to see. We must pastor each other. I have one man in my church who particularly pastors me, and we have deep conversations about spiritual things, which are vital to my life. We also go out for a curry sometimes!

As we get to know each other, we can be honest about our failures and problems, as well as the good things which are happening. It is vital to listen, as well as to speak, and integrity is paramount. I told a particular Christian confidentially of a need in my life, only to be asked about it by someone else in church the next Sunday. How did *they* know? I did not confide in that first Christian again. We must be trustworthy.

There should be such a strength in this faith-sharing with another believer. Both parties can move forward in their Christian lives as a result. We may have to take the initiative and then accept that it will not always work. A simple plea that you would benefit yourself from their support might be a way to begin.

Moving outwards

Sharing your faith with another Christian can have two further spin-offs:

- It need not be exclusive to two of you. You can include your spouses, your boy/girlfriends or your other close friends. A family can share their faith – as with praying together at breakfast before the day's work. Your example in faith-sharing with another Christian can encourage others to follow suit.

- It can open up many extra opportunities to share your faith together with those who need to come to faith. Look back to the charts in Key 5. Many of the people I surveyed said how much they wanted help from another Christian. On those charts, who would you have chosen to help you – and with whom could you then share your faith? You can only do this if you are faith-sharing with a Christian first. As they say, first find your Christian!

To end as I began this chapter, don't forget your own church leaders. Who does pastor your pastor? Who helps the vicar? Do the spiritual leaders ever get to share their faith with others? Do we let them give out so much that they get drained? Don't forget them – you could do a little faith-sharing there, too.

26 Drifters

For those over a certain age, I am not referring to the Drifters saving the last dance. (If you are young, ask your parents!) 'Drifters' are those people who have moved away from the Christian faith, and it would be great to see them back. How can we share our faith with them?

I have been working on this one myself recently: my own latest faith-sharing has been with four or five 'drifters'. In every other way these folk are doing well: they are only drifting from God. Two or three have, in fact, made deliberate moves away. I believe God wants them back. What can I do?

Be in touch

We Christians sometimes spurn, or ignore, those who go away from the Christian community, especially if they commit what we perceive to be a deliberate wrong. A couple of men I know left their Christian wives and families. They were dropped by us Christians like proverbial hot bricks. When I made contact, one told me no one had been in touch; the other said I was only the second Christian to speak with him in a year.

Of course there must be proper discipline exercised by the church leadership. Paul even speaks of handing people over 'to Satan' so they may have their 'spirit saved on the day of the Lord' (1 Corinthians 5:5). He quotes from Deuteronomy: 'Expel the wicked man from among you' (1 Corinthians 5:13). These are strong words! The church has often let evil remain within it, which is crazy. But when the person has gone, what then? If they have done wrong, should we leave them alone? And if they have not done wrong but have still drifted away, how should we react?

My biggest question is: what would Jesus do? I am a fan of Luke 15. Does the shepherd stick with the 99 'good' sheep, or go out looking for the one which has 'gone astray'? We know the answer. If no one else will make a move, why shouldn't I? Maybe I am stuck with being an evangelist, but I want to be out there looking, searching till I find.

How have I made contact? With one man in particular, I emailed him. His response was lukewarm, but he agreed to meet for coffee. He was very suspicious at first, but I explained myself in this way. I told him that he had been a good friend before he had left his wife and all of us at church. Like most men, I had no great collection of real friends, and I missed his friendship – which was the truth. I said I had no intention of preaching but simply wanted to keep our friendship going. I apologised that none of us had been in touch for the year. By expressing *my* need, he at once relaxed and said how glad he was to meet up again. When the prodigal son came home, his father showed his own delight. The shepherd did the same when he found the lost sheep.

Neutral ground is good. With each of the men I am re-befriending my initial meetings have been in coffee shops and pubs. It is where they feel comfortable (Key 6 may help here).

Talk

If ever I pray deeply, it is before – and during – these meetings. I really need the Holy Spirit's wisdom as to how and when to speak, and what to talk about (look back to Key 4). With two of these men, early on in our conversations I asked for forgiveness that I, and the rest of us, had kept our distance. I explained our embarrassment but said that was a poor excuse.

In every case there has been no need at all to accuse or to appear to preach. They know full well that they have made a bad move. What have we talked about? Many things. With one it has been football, with another my work, with a third his contacts with his wife and children. I have not had to force any spiritual conversation; it has come really naturally.

As we have parted after a chat over coffee or lunch, more than one asked me to pray for them. I was able to give four of them a book of daily Bible meditations for Christmas, which was welcomed and appreciated. Our conversations continue at a deep spiritual level.

I count it a great honour that these friends of mine, 'drifters' all, have allowed me to get alongside them. I am trusting God for his timing to help work things out. In every case we cannot go back – things have gone too far to rectify the past. But I believe we can go forward to God, the welcoming Father.

This has been a chapter very different from most, because it is extremely personal. I hope it is an encouragement. Please read Luke 15 again. Then go out looking for that lost sheep, however many are safely in the fold.

27 Next-door Neighbours

Earlier in this book I wrote about our next-door neighbours' tree. There it was, with a branch hanging down dangerously after a storm. I got permission from Mrs Next-door to cut it off, making life easier for Mr Next-door, with the happy consequence of an excellent relationship soon after we had moved in. If there is anyone (other than family) it would be good to get on with, it is them-next-door. More than that, it would be great to share our faith with them.

Be good!

Don't panic about this, but they are watching you. They can't help it. After all, you are watching them. That's because you are next door. Without making a big thing of it, they will be judging Christianity by what they see and hear generally, and you are probably the nearest example they have got. If you get it right, one or another could move into the 'friend' or even 'best friend' category, and those chapters would help. So look at Key 2, and get to know them.

In these days when people seem to live self-centred, isolated lives, it is not difficult to be a good neighbour. We got a Christmas card last year 'to the best neighbours in the world' – which was a vast exaggeration, but fantastic! If we can do it, you certainly should have no problem. My experience is that saying 'sorry' when appropriate is a great help!

There are all sorts of practical ways to share your faith. Volunteering to 'keep an eye open' when they are away is always valued. Time is vital – that chat over the fence, or when you put the bins out, or arrive home together. The opportunities are there, and should be taken, if only for a couple of minutes at a time. My wife is best at this. She makes time for a coffee with the wife on one side and the elderly widower on the other side. The latter especially appreciates this time to talk. I am much poorer at these contacts, but manage a once-in-a-while night-cap with this delightful older man.

Don't forget

We are so forgetful that we make lists. One of our lists is 'birthdays'. Our next-door neighbours are included and a card with a little present is really appreciated – and reciprocated. Obviously we also do this at Christmas, and we make an effort then, as well as at other times, for a 'come round for a mince pie/piece of birthday cake/(fill in your choice!)'.

We are occasionally horrified about how much time has elapsed since a last contact of real meaning. Do you ever have a meal with your next-door neighbours? What about a summer barbecue? They can smell it, whether invited or not! What is the relationship between the constituent members of your families: man-to-man, woman-to-woman, child-to-child? Don't force your young children to do more than they can cope with.

Should I say something?

Ask yourself, why not? There are two secrets:

- *Be natural.* Speak happily about where you go on Sunday mornings, why those cars are parked outside on a Tuesday evening when the home group meets (with apologies for thoughtless positioning across their drive!) and your church work. They will be interested. I have found times of crisis are a natural moment for saying that I will pray for whatever it is, and this is usually very much appreciated. I have stood with my older neighbour before taking him to hospital and seen the joy on his face when I offered to pray there and then.

- *Keep it light*. That prayer was gentle and short. Being 'heavy' is very bad news. I think the secret of faith-sharing next door is simply to be aware, and to take openings as they arise (Key 4). If you invite a neighbour to a meeting or a 'do' and they come – great! If not, accept graciously and go on being a good friend.

Be a positive, friendly, caring next-door neighbour. By so doing, you will be faith-sharing. After that, be natural in your speaking and sharing. It may take a long time, but don't lose heart and don't lose interest.

28 Other Neighbours

It is a sobering thought, but there are not all that many practising Christians around today. By having a Christian home on your street or in your block of flats, you may be the nearest Christian your neighbours see or know. I was talking with an older couple recently who said that the only Christian they knew was 'the grumpy old man over the road who goes to church'. What can we do here?

Be there

This is a recurring theme in this book, and the previous chapter on 'next-door' may give some pointers to general neighbourliness. Do any of our other neighbours feature in our priorities? Do we have, or make, any time for them? The answer is, very often, 'no'. Yet I have found, only recently, how the smallest gesture can work wonders.

The story is simple. I discovered that our post-lady was going to be 50 on her next birthday. All I did was get a big card and go round to about 20 neighbours getting them to sign it. Their reaction was fantastic. I had a happy chat with each one and was invited into several homes. It was an excellent 'getting to know you' exercise, and it either made or firmed-up friendships.

As with next-door neighbours, offers of practical help are a lovely way of witnessing to your neighbourhood. Would it help if you got a 'Neighbourhood Watch' going? Even if it were not 'official', your willingness to 'keep an eye out', take in the milk and the post, pay the window cleaner and so on is a positive way of demonstrating friendliness – as long as it is done in a non-pushy, non-sanctimonious way! If there are local issues, share the street's concerns. Parking restrictions, refuse collection times – we have talked about these with our neighbours, and helped to get them sorted out. Your street or block of flats will have united problems sometimes, and your Christian faith should not only have something to say but a Christ-like way of saying it.

Take the opportunities

When it comes to saying something, what can be done?

- *Christmas cards.* Don't be dreadfully unsubtle, but there are some great Christian cards. We are always interested by how many of our neighbours send us 'Christian' cards in return!
- *Be aware of happy occasions* (weddings, new babies) and major sorrows (bereavements, marriage failures). A card, and an appropriate comment, is much better than saying nothing. When our Indian neighbours had a wedding recently, the father was delighted when I wandered up the road to congratulate him and the family on their daughter's happiness.
- *Do remember our 'New Year's Day Breakfast'* as a great neighbourhood possibility (see Key 2).
- *A summer barbecue*, a mince pie at Christmas – what would your neighbours value? It need not involve alcohol, if that is a problem. Some of your neighbours (including members of some other faiths) would prefer a cup of tea.

From 'doing' to talking

You are Christ's ambassador where you live. Your presence speaks of him – well or badly. Should you say anything? Here are two thoughts:

- In the context of the disciples visiting a town, Jesus spoke of homes where 'peace' could rest (Matthew 10:11–12). Ask God to show you homes like that in your neighbourhood, where his good news would be welcome. His Holy Spirit will lead you. Your friendship will lead naturally into conversations about Jesus.
- Look carefully for opportunities, and take them when they arise (Key 4). If you are positive about being a good neighbour, don't be shy about speaking of your faith in Jesus when it is clear that you should. Time, concern and willingness are the keys. You can help some of your neighbours meet Jesus. Pray for openings. Your neighbourhood is the 'Jerusalem' of your own mission field (Acts 1:8). Have the courage, and the 'compassion' (Matthew 9:36), to go for it.

29 Outside Helpers

'With whom would you like to share your faith?' The survey I conducted produced answers which included 'the roof man', 'my hairdresser' and 'the cobbler'. To these I would add: what about the post lady, the bin men, the window cleaner, the shop assistant, the dentist and the nurse at the doctor's surgery? You will have to add to these your own contacts. Can we share our faith with them? How?

Be kind

'Be nice to me, I'm having a hard day.' Many people feel like that. If you can be kind to those who help you, you may be surprised how much of an impact that will have as a positive way to share your Christian faith. Similarly, the words 'thank you' work wonders. When I have written letters of thanks, I have often had grateful replies.

Kindness can be expressed in several ways. Don't be mean at Christmas if a gift is appropriate. Help the person to help you. The roof man will appreciate a cuppa, the hairdresser will be glad if you turn up on time and the window cleaner will be grateful to be able to use your tap for his bucket. Your understanding will also prove positive: for example *not* keeping them talking when they have a living to earn.

The simple acknowledgement of these busy workers, and gratitude for what they do, will be the exception to the rule these days. Act, and react, with the love of Christ, and you will be sharing your faith without even realising it. It will be noticed, and noted.

Who are they?

Is the person in this category a 'worker' or a person? Is it 'the post lady' or 'Mary'? Is it 'the roof man' or 'Bill'? Are they just people doing a job, or do you care about them as individuals precious to God? This is another time to look at Key 2. Those who answered my survey by mentioning, for example, 'the cobbler', clearly had that person on their hearts. If you feel that way about someone who helps you, be sure to have them in your prayers, asking God for opportunities to share your faith with them.

Take an interest in them as people. I mentioned in the last chapter how I went round our neighbours to get a card signed for our post-lady's birthday. She was so thrilled! A small gesture like that takes minimal effort. Think 'What can I do?' before 'What should I say?' Now let's look at that.

Just a word

You may well be a small stepping stone for someone in this chapter. There is every chance that *they* will say something about your faith, because it will be shining through. When they ask, don't preach, but don't give a half-hearted answer either. With some there may be time to talk. Hairdressers are chatty people. The roof man may come down for a coffee and a biscuit, and stand around with you.

Look for heaven-sent openings. I walked into my dentist's waiting room a couple of days before writing this. His 'muzak' was playing an orchestral version of 'Amazing Grace'. My dentist (Steve) knows I am an evangelist, and we often talk of my trips to Africa (when my mouth is not full of his drill). I jokingly asked him if he now had personalised music for all his patients and said how impressed I had been to hear 'Amazing Grace' playing just for me! It went down very well. It was a Key 4 moment – time for 20 seconds of happy Christian witness – then on to the drilling.

Faith-sharing is just that – sharing our faith by deed and word, by being instruments of God's love. We may not lead 'the cobbler' to Christ, but we can help him come nearer. He, and the others who fall within the context of this chapter, are people sent across our paths. The right action, the right word, at the right time, is what they need.

30 Inside Helpers

In the survey, 'the cleaner' was one answer given to the question 'With whom would you like to share your faith?' This might include other people who come to our home, such as 'the home help', our child minder, or someone, like a nurse or health visitor, who attends a needy family member.

A Christian home

The obvious thing here is to have an environment where Jesus lives. What sort of picture does that conjure up for you? For me, it would be a place of fun and happiness, of acceptance and love. It would not be stuffy, boring or sanctimonious! Nor is it a place of complete perfection, but rather a home of joyful learning about how to get it right. Faith-sharing is visible before it is oral.

In your home you are allowed to have standards. Many homes would have a 'no smoking' policy these days. In the same way, you will want to choose carefully those you employ to help you. In particular, a child minder is playing a crucial role in that early life development. You will be well thought of for having and maintaining these positive rules.

When it is known that you are a Christian, whoever is alongside you in your home will be watching you. Don't be scared! Simply live and behave as a friend of Jesus. Avoid being 'corny' – there is no need to leave 'helpful' Christian literature around! Whoever the person is, be good to them.

This does not mean letting them take unfair advantage of your kindness, but a word of thanks, a cuppa, a remembered birthday, an 'extra' at Christmas, all speak of your Christian concern.

Saying something

Just because someone is working with you and for you in your home does not give you the right to preach at them. Far from it – they are almost a captive audience and thus any undue pressure would be very wrong. The secret is, once again, in Key 2: you must earn the right to speak of your faith. They may not mind if you do chat – after all, you are paying!

Can you talk about Jesus quite naturally? A coffee break is the obvious time. If the person is a paid visitor (a nurse or a social worker for example), their time may be of the essence to them, so don't delay them. Even with the cleaner, there is work to be done. Happy chatting is the way. Be interested in them and talk about their interests before yours. Enthuse about your church and your Christian friends and activities. The child minder will want to know what you do with the child yourself, prayers at bedtime included.

If the helper is of the opposite sex, do be careful to keep things on a business-like footing. If you become friends, it will help to refer to that chapter. Be aware of problems and crises the person may have, and don't be afraid to say you will be praying for them.

My mother was brilliant with our home helps over the years. Each one was really encouraged spiritually through a quiet, natural faith-sharing. More than one came to know Jesus Christ, and others came much closer to him. Mum was no preacher; in fact she was a very quiet Christian. Perhaps that was the secret: her knowing Jesus was so attractive that the cleaner lady found her faith irresistible. They would chat as they sorted out the kitchen, and no conversation was ever forced. No wonder those ladies would work for her for years!

Sensitivity and a gentle style: that is the secret here. Share your faith with your home helpers naturally and positively. Let the Holy Spirit open the door for you.

31 Cult Visitors

Here they come, door-knocking down the street, smartly dressed enough to be obvious. It's the JWs (Jehovah's Witnesses), or the Mormons, or some other off-centre sect. They are our neighbours for a brief moment. What should we do about our faith-sharing here? After all, they want to do that with us.

Non-involvement

Do you want to get into a faith-sharing conversation with cult members? You can share your faith with a smile and a gentle refusal. I have a friend who is a vicar. Why the JWs go to the vicarage is beyond me, but they do. Here is his standard conversation:

'We've come to interest you in the Bible' (imagine that as an opener to a vicar!).

'Ah – you're JWs.'

'Never mind that, we want . . .'

'Well that proves it! Now I'm not going to talk with you, but I am going to pray for you.'

At that point he puts his hands on their shoulders and prays out loud for the two of them (they always come in pairs). As you would guess, they are shocked! They either stand still or walk away. If they walk, he goes with them to the gate, still praying. He prays that God will open their hearts to the truth and that, to prove his reality, he will give them no success at all that day. Then he says goodbye. It is a novel approach!

If you don't feel competent enough to tackle the Moonies, Christian Scientists, Christadelphians, Mormons, JWs or whomever, have a plan to say something positive when you say 'no'.

Telling it straight

Whoever your callers are, they have come to share their faith, so all previous rules about 'earning the right' are out of the window. You are in it from the word go.

What do you know about them?

Get your minister to lend you a book on what the main cults believe, or pay a visit to your nearest Christian bookshop. You need to question whether the Bible has been added to (e.g. the Book of Mormon). Do they believe Jesus was both completely human and divine? Do you have to work to gain your salvation (as the JWs do)? How sure are you of your own faith? A serious look at Key 1 may be a good idea. If the visitor represents a more 'Eastern' religion, you will need to look up what the Bible says about death and judgement (no reincarnation), Jesus as the *only* Son of God, the reality of sin, and God as a *person*.

How should you behave?

Take it easy – this is not warfare, and not the place for physical or even verbal aggression. Relax and have a sense of humour. Whatever you do, do not have a 'crack' at their false beliefs and, in particular, their organisation. These are people for whom Jesus died, and your caring Christian witness will speak volumes. These cult followers are searching for God themselves. In their hearts, though not their words, they are not sure. They are deeply suspicious of you as a 'Christian', and your being nice will work wonders.

What should you say?

You will need to listen first. Then ask if you can share your own experience, and speak of how wonderful it is to have a personal relationship with Jesus. Whatever they have, they do not have the inner witness of the Holy Spirit, nor the assurance of sins forgiven or a place in heaven. Try to keep to these central issues: red herrings about how many are going to be in heaven are not helpful. Their version of the Bible may be differently worded from yours.

Keep asking yourself, 'What is my aim?' It should not be to win points! It must be to help them to know Jesus. They do not need to be mocked, but rather helped to think through the truth about Jesus, his love for them and the change he can make. Like my friend the vicar, say you will pray for them, even if you don't do it there and then. (And remember to pray after they have gone!) Invite them back, if appropriate. You could be a stepping-stone to a cult member coming into real faith. It will certainly test your own.

32 Passers-by

I was building a little garden wall by the pavement. I am no DIY expert, and it was taking ages. An older lady walked up the road as I was kneeling with a brick in one hand and a trowel in the other. I looked up. 'Say one for me!' she said as she saw me kneeling, and smiled as she said it.

Is it possible to share our faith with passers-by or those we pass by as we walk the dog in the park or wander along the street?

Take your time

In a world of rushing about, who has time to smile and say 'hello'? Who bothers, even if they do have time? You do! At least, I hope you do. If your life consists of charging around in a semi-demented frenzy, this category is not for you. Galloping round the park with the dog, or ripping out weeds in the garden as if there were no tomorrow, will miss the moment with the passer-by. My wall was not being built in a day. I smiled back at the lady's joking request and replied, 'I will!' An hour later, when she returned with her shopping, I told her, 'I did!' (because I had prayed for her as she disappeared towards town). It made my Saturday – and by the look on her face, it made hers.

That was faith-sharing. So is being cheerful in poor weather, or giving God the credit when the park glows with flowers. It does not mean going over the top with an ultra-pious style. Nor does it mean taking leave of your senses and being over-friendly with the opposite sex – or even the same sex – in a rather lonely park. Parks can be dangerous places, and your innocent overtures may be misconstrued.

Take your moment

Apart from being generally friendly, you are not going to be able to do very much faith-sharing with more than one or two. Even then, your opportunities may be limited. Most people will fall into images, like 'the man in the jogging bottoms with the retriever', or 'the woman who pulls a little shopping trolley'. However, one or two people will begin to feature regularly. A smile from the front garden and a 'hello' to an older couple going shopping, a pause with another dog owner as your dogs do a little mutual admiring (I put that delicately!), and you soon get to know people. 'My dog is in love with your dog!' I was informed (rather worryingly) a few days ago.

It is a getting-to-know-you process (Key 2). Is the Holy Spirit leading you here (Key 3)? Is there an opportunity to sit on the front wall, or on a park bench, or to walk the dogs together (Key 6)? See how the conversation goes, and don't leave God out. It may be a one-liner, as mine was with that older lady. Seeds are sown that way.

If the relationship develops, you can refer to the sections on 'other neighbours' and 'friends'. Here is someone who could be invited to your 'New Year's Day Breakfast', or a Christmas mince pie. Your local church may have a special event at Easter, Harvest or Christmas, for example. A few invitations to 'Carols by Candlelight' could be given out while sauntering round the park. If, later, you find one screwed up, pop it in the bin! But – who knows? – 'See you there?' might do the trick.

Not every section in this book is going to lead necessarily to a 'conversion'. This may be one category where your demeanour is your faith-sharing: your smile shows God's love; your one sentence is a tiny help along the way. I am sure my prayer for that lady was heard and answered, although I have no idea how. But I'm glad I've written this chapter, because I wanted to show that we can share Christ's love with anyone, whatever the outcome.

33   The Housebound

Here is a wonderful category for faith-sharing! You may want to look at the next category as well, as many who are housebound are ill. But that is not always so, hence this chapter.

Giving time

An early decision needs to be made here: have you got enough time for those who are housebound? A one-off visit will always be appreciated, but anything meaningful will mean an ongoing relationship. Is this a commitment you can undertake?

Your faith-sharing will have a major practical element here. There is shopping to be done. You may be able to arrange transport for outings, trips to church, the countryside, the shops, the pub or wherever. In so doing, make sure you don't usurp what the person's family members feel is their domain. Nor should you try to upstage the social services and health services. Furthermore, be sure not to make yourself vulnerable, or put yourself in compromising situations.

However, your loving, caring attitude will enable your faith to shine through. Make the chores seem fun and, where possible, do things *with* the housebound rather than *for* them.

Chatting

There will be very many opportunities for talking about a host of subjects. Chat naturally about anything and everything. Reminiscing will be a regular feature. Talk about your own life and your story: Key 3 is worth revisiting. Share about your personal relationship with Jesus quite naturally as the opportunity arises (Key 4). What has happened in your personal life does matter and is interesting – even if you don't think so!

Equally, listen to their story. Knowing your Christian connections, they may well speak of spiritual influences and events in their life. Don't be afraid to ask kind questions: a conversational style is much better than a series of monologues. It shows you are listening and have a keen interest. Again with reference to Key 3, let the Holy Spirit help your moving forward here.

As you feel you are making progress in what may be long and ongoing conversations, you could volunteer to read to your housebound friend. Would they like to hear from the Bible? You could say how you enjoy a daily time with God, and see if that leads to sharing that time with them. Suggest sensitively that you would be happy to pray with them and for them – perhaps as you are about to leave.

The housebound often have periods of being on their own. An offer of an easy-going Christian book, or some CDs, might go down well. This is certainly one of those situations where you can be gently proactive. If there is a genuinely sympathetic reaction, move forward with them. Who knows? You may be the one to help them find their own faith (Key 7).

Other help

What is your church's policy regarding the housebound? Does it have one? Are there visitors appointed by the church? Does your church take Holy Communion to people in their homes? Is there a transport co-ordinator? When you have answers to these questions, you can offer any extra help that may be needed.

Similarly, would your housebound friend appreciate being taken to your church's service or mid-week meeting? Does your church hold events for those who are housebound, or for those in the age group of your housebound neighbour? Would you be willing to run one?

The potential for faith-sharing here is very great indeed. It is worth all the time and effort. The old prayer says that 'it is in giving that we receive'. You can give and receive a blessing in your faith-sharing with the housebound.

34 The Sick

'I was sick and you looked after me,' Jesus said in Matthew 25:36 when encouraging us to care for others. I love the style of Jesus, going out of his way to be with people who are ill. The man lying by the pool in John 5:1–15 is a splendid example. Of all our neighbours, perhaps this last group needs us most. The previous chapter on the housebound is worth reading first.

Helping

People who are ill are unlikely to phone and say, 'Come and see me.' You will have to take the initiative to show concern. This may prove time-consuming. Are you willing to keep on with your contact after they are discharged from hospital and then have a long period of recuperation, or as they fail to make a reasonable recovery from a stroke? Picking people up and then metaphorically dropping them does not speak well of our faith.

As with the housebound, your faith will be seen in the practical help you give. You may be the scribe in writing to family and friends, or the shopper for those necessities (best be a woman for certain feminine items – or a brave man!). Transport to and from hospital and doctors' appointments could feature.

Sharing

It is my experience that times of illness are very special opportunities to take the initiative in speaking of our faith and of the help Jesus longs to give. Without needing to be at all pushy, here is what may prove to be a unique opening to share God's love and concern for the one who is ill, whatever is wrong. Indeed, I would go so far as to say that, unless it seems a positively *bad* idea, I would always offer to pray with and for someone I was visiting who was ill. I cannot understand an ordained minister ever failing to do this. People have said to me, after a minister has visited, 'I wish he'd prayed for me.'

I have done some research into those suffering from strokes and dementia, and also have had personal experience of friends and family with these problems. Who knows what they can understand? My stepmother suffered for several years from a serious stroke. She could hardly complete a sentence on many occasions, yet she prayed beautifully and fluently. She taught me that we can share deep spiritual matters, albeit in an uncomplicated language, and cut through the physical and mental barriers right into the depths of the heart and soul. Speak of God's love to stroke and dementia sufferers because he can work where no one else can. Those who suffer from mental illness should be treated in a similar way.

My only caveat is to be careful if others are present. Otherwise, speak of Jesus and his willingness to be right there in the suffering. I hold hands with a sick person – male or female, young or old – unless it seems inappropriate. I almost always hold their hand, or gently place a hand on their shoulder, when praying.

Visiting in institutions

If your neighbour or friend is ill or frail enough to be in a hospital, nursing home or hospice, there could well be others around, so particular sensitivity is needed. I always phone first, to see if my visit is convenient both for the staff and the person I wish to see. If I say I am 'from the church', that sometimes opens doors, especially to get me in when others (including family) may not be there. These days, visiting is allowed at most times. If your sick friend is in the institution for a long time, the chapter on the housebound is relevant. For a person in a nursing home, that may well be their home, and the same applies to a hospice.

I try to ignore the medical paraphernalia! I chat about the happenings in the world, especially those which will interest my sick neighbour. I keep the conversation light and happy. My aim is to find out how my sick neighbour really is, now they are in this place. They are clearly poorly enough to be in a hospital or hospice, or not strong enough to go to their own home, hence the nursing home. It is obvious they are physically unwell. But what about their spiritual health?

I trust God for an opening in the conversation to talk about God, his love and his concern. After that, it is simply a case of following the leading of the Holy Spirit and sharing Jesus in a naturally easy-going way. If the nurse walks in with the tablets, we suspend the chat until medication time is over – then we go on! It would be wholly exceptional for me to leave without praying. In any bigger institution there is almost certainly a chaplain. I would encourage my sick neighbour to make contact, if I could not do so myself. They also could have a real role to play in helping with spiritual matters.

I do believe that these visits – when a person is ill enough to be in a hospital, hospice or nursing home – are very special opportunities for sharing in a positive way the love of Jesus. It is another of those situations where I would aim to 'go for it'. The following story sums up how I feel.

My dying neighbour

A neighbour of mine was extremely ill in hospital. I knew him well. He was a leading churchman. I went to see him one morning and asked him directly how his faith was helping him. Tears ran down his face. 'It's all in my head,' he said. 'It doesn't make any difference now.'

I held his hand and read the first few verses of John 14, where Jesus speaks of being the only way to the Father and says that he has prepared a place for us. I asked my dying neighbour if he would trust Jesus. We prayed together. A fortnight later I went to his funeral, but my sorrow was not filled with hopelessness. God gave me that one opportunity – I am so glad I took it. Your sick neighbour may not be in such dire straits, but their illness may still be the open door for positive faith-sharing. Let God take you through that door.

35 The Boss

Work in the twenty-first century seems a far cry from Bruce Forsyth's 'I'm in charge!' (which you need to be older to remember) and even further from 'Slaves, obey your earthly masters' (Ephesians 6:5). But there is a hierarchy in most jobs, so how can we share our faith with those who are in authority over us at work?

A good worker

'Serve wholeheartedly, as if you were serving the Lord' is how Paul puts it in Ephesians 6:7. The 'boss' is watching and will see your faith in your good and enthusiastic work and your positive attitude towards it. Your Christian presence in your workplace is significant. Are you the calm in the storm, showing God's presence and his love?

The boss, and those who are above you on 'the ladder of success', are almost certainly living under pressure. They often live with the fear of failure and the threat of redundancy, or falling profits and not being able to deliver. Your aim, as a Christian, is to help them do a good job. Of course you are not to let the boss walk all over you, but there has to be a 'respect' (Ephesians 6:5) and a 'sincerity' (Colossians 3:22) from you to them.

In a working world where secular standards dominate, your Christian style will shine through. This is genuine faith-sharing and any words will depend on this.

A thoughtful sharer

Does the management team know you are a Christian? The best way is to tell one of them simply, positively and enthusiastically. The news will get round. Finding a suitable moment needs tact (Key 4), but the sooner the better. You may well find that the hierarchy contains one or two fellow believers.

After that, your faith-sharing may be predominantly reactive, unless it is very clear that you should take the lead. One instance is in situations of work or personal crisis, when a quiet 'I'm praying' may be appreciated. A number of my friends have told their bosses of their Christian concern when the boss has confided that there were difficulties at home, or there was a particularly hard meeting to face and the expression 'Say one for me' was less of a joke and more of a genuine plea.

If the boss wants to talk, then go for it. He or she is giving tacit permission for their time to be used in that way. Apart from that, you need to be asking others in leadership positions who are Christians what they are doing for those at management level. Do they hold breakfast or lunch meetings? Many towns do, so why not yours? Ask them to invite your boss. Does your workplace have a Christian fellowship or a gathering for prayer? When I worked for the Coventry City Council we had a prayer gathering in the Council Chamber every Monday morning to pray for our city, our leaders, our superiors and our colleagues.

The best faith-sharing with the boss is to work well, show the peace of Christ and be ready always to offer his love. Pray for the opportunities and take them when they come.

36 Your Staff

How can you share your faith with those who work under your supervision, especially those who work most closely for you?

A good boss

Here is a good starter: 'Masters, provide your slaves with what is right and fair, because you know that you have a Master in heaven' (Colossians 4:1). In this enlightened century, 'masters' may well be female, and 'slaves' is far gone – or is it? We shall see. However, you are in charge, so beware exerting undue pressure, especially if you want to share your faith.

As the person in charge, your Christianity will shine through the way you respect and appreciate your staff. I believe we are in danger of allowing a new slavery in many of our workplaces. We expect workers – often at senior levels – to work ridiculously long hours. I heard recently of a young female lawyer going home at 8.30 p.m. and being told by the senior partner, 'If you think you're going to get on in this firm, you'll have to work longer than this.' Poor girl, where was her life on the outside?

A Christian boss will not want to be overfamiliar, especially with members of the opposite sex, but will want to show a genuine interest in the staff. Are you aware of the pressures they feel when they are continually overloaded with work or, conversely, often feel underused and little valued? If it is within your power, do you ensure they have good conditions of service, including reasonable pay? I am aware of so-called 'Christian' firms that pay the lowest rates and whose ethical practices are questionable. Our style of management speaks volumes of our faith.

A caring sharer

If you are going to speak of your faith, Keys 2 and 4 are vital. How well do you know your assistant or your staff? For example, if they have a crisis at home, will they receive your sympathy and a quiet offer of prayer? Will a time to speak of God's love arise naturally, through the good relationship you have as you talk of other things? An awareness of joys and sorrows will open doors.

In the heavy pressure of work, does your team sense the peace of God ruling your heart? And, when it does not, would they ever receive a 'sorry'? Believe it or not, your assistant may be a bit scared of you! You may need to take the lead in making conversation, or in helping the atmosphere to be relaxed enough to allow questions and comments about spiritual matters. Without being corny, do you give thoughtful cards and presents at birthdays and Christmas? Even words like 'Have a brilliant Christmas – God bless you!' can make a difference.

Like any other relationship, you need to earn the right to speak. But a genuine joy when mentioning a great church service, or speaking of something God has done for you, can come quite naturally out of 'How was the weekend?' A throwaway sentence ('I felt such joy in worship at church yesterday') will say so much.

The previous and the next two chapters may help as well. Like a next-door neighbour, you could be the only Christian your member of staff knows. Be open to the Holy Spirit's leading, and share your faith well.

37 Fellow Workers

Whether it be in an office, a shop, a factory, a school or on a farm, there are people who work alongside us. What can we do about faith-sharing here? Please refer to the last two chapters on Christian behaviour at work – then we can get into open faith-sharing immediately.

Be positive

As in most situations in this book, Key 2 applies: how well do you know your work colleagues? And how well do they know you? There is a section in Key 8 about helping a new Christian to witness to their faith: check back to it now. It will help all your faith-sharing if the folk at work know you are a genuine, normal Christian. Forget the soap-box style – a quiet word with someone who tells everyone the latest news will do fine.

Beware of assuming what they think. I heard of a man who decided he would never speak of his faith but wait for an opening. After ten years, a work colleague said, 'You know, there's something different about you.' 'Yes!' he replied eagerly. 'No, don't tell me,' his colleague replied. 'I know what it is – you're a vegetarian!' Ten years of silence, only to be misidentified. I hope the story is apocryphal.

While you are not paid to chat, there are situations where faith-sharing can be a natural part of togetherness, so don't rush off for a Christian meeting every lunchtime, or go home for lunch every day, or shop alone. In conversation, be positive about your faith; we have to get away from the boring concept that Christians are the ones who love to say 'no'! For example, if you don't want to join in the office raffle, give a donation to the charity concerned instead. Be the life and soul of the office party, without getting smashed. Jesus went to some fairly lively parties with those he worked with – and they loved him (as in Matthew 9:10).

If someone wants to have a crack at you for your faith, often because someone in the wider church has brought unfortunate publicity on Christianity, take their sniping in good heart, with a smile and a genuine apology for clear wrongdoing. Reacting in a kind, positive and happy way will win the day. If you are seen to be irked you will be the loser.

Be ready

As I said in the chapter 'Other Neighbours', there will be people 'of peace' at work, who will have a real interest in the things of God. They will be glad you are a Christian and, as you discover who they are, it will be very natural for you to share your faith with them. In a similar way, certain events will lend themselves to your saying something. In my very first job, one of our leading members of staff died. The whole office walked to the church for her funeral. It was a unique day, and the conversation was deeply spiritual. Without any pushing, I established a completely different relationship with two or three work colleagues, and we never looked back. One of them ultimately became a Christian – not directly through me, but his journey to faith began that day.

One very positive way of faith-sharing is to have a Christian group at work. One of my sons sent an internal memo round the firm where he was a junior member, asking if anyone would like to contact him about a Christian group. He got several positive replies, and they met weekly to pray and to study God's word together. I have visited many offices and factories to speak at their Christian group's carol service, with very many work colleagues present. These groups are not only helping the Christians to live for Christ at work, but can hold excellent 'open' events where a visiting speaker, or one of their own number, can encourage others to know Christ.

A tough cookie

I worked in one office where a colleague delighted in hammering me for being a Christian. He enjoyed getting at me in front of others. He openly derided my faith. One day during lunch, he physically grabbed me and pulled me into an empty room and locked the door. I thought I was dead!

'Ian,' he said, 'I need your help. My wife and I are having our first baby. We know we've got to do something about God for our child. You're the only Christian I know. Tell me what to do.'

As they say, you could have knocked me down with a feather! We had an amazing conversation and were great friends thereafter. Take heart: even the toughest need you to be a Christian. Who knows when your day will come to share your faith?

38 Those Who Serve

This little chapter is about those who are often the 'slave labour' of an office, a school or a factory: the cleaner, the post boy, the members of the typing pool, the courier and so on. Who shares their faith with them? How can you do that? Here are a few ideas.

Be kind

Most places of work are tough and demanding. It is easy for those at the bottom of the workforce to become non-persons, doers of jobs, there to be kicked if things go wrong. What can we do for them so that our Christianity impacts their lives?

- *Treat them as people*. They have tough, repetitive work to do, which can be boring and seem meaningless. We can encourage them with words and actions that help them to see their value.
- *We can smile*. It seems a small thing, but a peaceful, kindly, caring approach will be rare for them.
- *For the postroom*: don't send 50 letters to be dealt with five minutes before closing!
- *For the laboratory assistant*: your mess is his or her problem. Try not to make it impossible.
- *For the typing pool*: be grateful. I once worked in a large office where everyone shared a typing pool. We rarely saw the typists, but sent our work on dictated tapes via the office 'runner'. When I left, the pool's head said to me,

'We're going to miss you. You're the only one who says "thank-you" at the end of each tape.' I thought it was a normal thing to do – but apparently not.

- *Be polite* to the phone operator, especially ten minutes after work has started and everyone wants their call *NOW*! The pressure is enormous.
- *Ease the burden* by helping each 'server' along, so the senior hierarchy keep off their backs.

You see what I am suggesting? We Christians should be the encouragers, the affirmers of people who work 'for' us. Our faith will be shared through our caring style and be very visible and appreciated.

Be available

As in several other chapters, it is important that servers know we are true Christians. If the workplace generally knows, they will know, because the servers know most things that are going on. By your attitude and style, they need to realise you are 'there' for them. This is all part of Key 2, as you get to know each other. The right time (Key 4) to say something will arise in God's time.

An appreciative gift at Christmas, and a card then and at birthdays, is a kind move. Is your ear close enough to the ground to hear of any personal work problems they might have? Your help and concern at times of difficulty is crucial, and may prove the door-opener for sharing your faith verbally as at no other time. It may be, with these servers, that you will have little opportunity to be anything other than one small link in their spiritual lives. But your style of treating them well will have a real influence. Here is a way to show the compassion of Jesus. If he shines through you, they will be blessed. That is faith-sharing.

39 Teachers

This chapter is for those at school or college. What about your teachers and lecturers: how should you share your faith with them?

Mission impossible?

You may be thinking: 'I've looked at Key 5, and there are too many problems here.' You may be right! For example:

- You may be very young compared with your teachers, so they would not be willing to listen to you.
- They might think you were showing off, or trying to 'suck up' to them.
- At college, the teaching staff are often very 'distant' from the students, and there is little personal contact.

But – you want to know what *is* possible: so here goes.

Some possibilities

- Be a Christian! As you live, with Jesus helping you, your teachers will notice. That is the first way to share your faith with them, and may be the most important.
- Your school, especially if you are at junior school, will celebrate religious festivals. As and when you get the chance, you can say why the Christian ones matter to you. Easter is especially good, and so is Christmas.
- Be enthusiastic about the Christian things you do outside

school. When a teacher asks, 'What did you do at the weekend?' and you want to tell them about your fantastic Christian group at church, don't be afraid or ashamed to do so. In the same way, you can be excited about the holiday club, going to a Christian summer camp or house party, attending a brilliant festival like New Wine, Spring Harvest or Easter People, or going to a fabulous Christian concert. Everyone else tells the teacher what they have enjoyed: why not you?

- If your church is putting on a really good 'special', why not invite your teacher to come? It would be particularly good if you, and others from school, were doing something in the event or service.

- Do you have a Christian group in your school or college? Look at the next-but-one chapter which talks about this. But, as far as your teacher is concerned, he or she might even like to join in from time to time, or come to an extra-special meeting you all put on. By some of the things your group does you can show that you all, as Christians, care for the other pupils, the teachers, the school and the needy world outside.

- Whatever you feel you can't do, you *can* pray for your teachers. They often have a tough job, and God can bless them. He wants to! If you realise that your teacher is having a particularly hard time, find a quiet moment to say, 'I prayed for you last night.' You may be surprised how pleased he or she will be to know that.

It is very unlikely you will be able to say very much to your teacher about your faith in a direct way. But if you try these ideas, you will help your teacher to know of God's love, and you will encourage them to realise that they need Jesus too.

40 Pupils

This is a chapter for teachers. Here are a few thoughts on faith-sharing for you.

Take care

Yours is a unique situation. Teachers have enormous influence over children, especially younger ones. You must therefore be careful not to abuse the powerful and privileged position which is yours. On the other hand, if you have looked at the earlier chapters on children and teenagers, you will know how far away from any Christian influences the vast majority of our young people appear to be. You may be the only Christian many of your pupils know, and you can have a major impact on their spiritual lives. You should be aware of this, and be available to help the children in your classes.

I am sure you will take the utmost care in any counselling situations, especially one-to-one, making sure you are in full view of another adult at all times. We all know of dreadful accusations made by pupils and parents which have ruined colleagues' lives. Be very careful to act wisely at all times.

Be positive

Be a great teacher! Be good, fair, firm, consistent and kind; a real Christian in all you do and say. In your teaching, you will want to respect other faiths and avoid proselytising.

However, you can be positive about the Bible and the Christian faith: the law allows and encourages this. While you have no right to 'preach', you are able to say what you personally believe and have found to be true.

Do enthuse about major Christian festivals such as Christmas and Easter. If you teach scientific subjects, you will be glad to know that many scientists are Christians who do not find the Bible inconsistent with their work. Music, art and poetry abound in matters 'true . . . noble . . . right . . . pure . . . lovely . . . admirable' (Philippians 4:8). Be happily positive about your faith, and there will be no need to push it.

Share

A word about parents: you will inevitably establish a close relationship with some, and they may value your Christian approach. If you have the time, and the Holy Spirit leads, be available to help them spiritually where appropriate.

For your pupils, whatever else you do not do, you can pray for them. A number of my teacher friends have colleagues with whom they pray regularly. One school (at least) in the city where I live has a teachers' Christian fellowship. At another, Christian staff meet to pray once a week at the school at 7.30 a.m. – sacrificial but hugely worthwhile.

Speaking of fellowships, could you help Christian pupils start their own Christian Union? (The next chapter is about this.) In a junior school you will need to organise this. Again, I know of brilliant groups run by, or with, Christian teachers. The group will be purely voluntary, and needs to be at a good time to enable attendance (lunchtimes work well). In one school I know, staff and pupil Christian fellowships join together from time to time. If your church is near the school, encourage the minister to get involved in the school and to put on events which will appeal to staff and pupils. If the church has good youth and children's activities, these can be made known (again without pushing).

It is my experience that a Christian teacher can have a wonderful influence for good in a school, as the love of Jesus shines through and attracts pupils to God. You may not be the last link in the chain, but you could be the first. Let's face it: you have dozens more opportunities each day than your minister does in a week! Share your faith sensitively, and many pupils will be blessed.

41 Christian Unions

Do you have a Christian fellowship where you work? Faith-sharing can and should be a 'together' activity. You will have seen the chapter on sharing your faith with another Christian, followed by the one on drifters. It can be tough to be a Christian at work, so why not help each other?

'Work' is where you work (obviously), so I include here those who go to school (pupils and teachers), as well as workers in factories, department stores or offices, etc. – indeed, anywhere where there are two or three Christians working together. What can you do together to share your faith?

Get going

Why not have a Christian Union or fellowship? (It's yours, so call it what you will.) For office workers, look back to 'Fellow Workers' to see how my son got his going. You will have a pretty good idea of one or two other Christians in your workplace (school included). Simply ask them if they would join you for a chat to plan the where/when/how/who of a Christian group.

There is no reason why a school should not have one group for teachers and another for pupils. It would be great in all other workplaces if staff at all levels could meet together – management and workers, the 'white' and 'blue' collars, are equal as Christians! If you need permission, approach the manager or headteacher, especially as you will need a room.

The advantages

Why are you doing this? I'm sure you can add to these:

- Christians can be such an encouragement to each other in the workplace. Pray for each other and study the Bible to deepen your faith.
- The workplace will be blessed through your prayers and your positive Christian approach to how you work together.
- When crises come, your group can be at the forefront of positive answers. For example, at one nearby school, the father of a pupil had a near-death road accident. The staff and pupil Christian Unions joined together for a united prayer time the following lunch hour. Many dozens of other staff and pupils joined them, including non-believers and members of other faiths, such was the concern for the father. The whole school was glad at the lead taken.
- The Christian group can put on occasional events which will help others who are interested to consider Christianity (see under next heading).
- Those who are not sure of their faith can be part of the group (as can non-Christians), and discover a real assurance of knowing Jesus. Your group must cater for all churches and all church backgrounds.

What to do

It's your group, so work it out together! But do make it really enjoyable – the best part of the working week. A few ideas:

- In a junior school, a Christian teacher will be crucial for leadership.
- In a senior school, if a teacher is involved, it is very important to let pupils take the lead.

- On a weekly basis, the group is to help the Christians to grow. Why not start with some easy-to-do studies in (say) Mark's Gospel, and a time of open prayer? Share on a rota who leads each week.
- For schools, get all the help you can from Scripture Union's school workers, and from Youth for Christ. They both can advise, visit sometimes, and encourage. For colleges, contact UCCF (Universities and Colleges Christian Fellowship) if there is no Christian Union yet.
- Apart from in times of crisis, which are unplanned(!), do have some brilliant 'open' occasions. You could put on a charity 'famine' lunch, support a good cause, get a speaker who can really communicate with your colleagues, show a video – there are many opportunities.
- Make a big thing of Christmas. Put on a really good carol service, with splendid refreshments and a speaker who will give a short and meaningful talk.
- In, or before, Holy Week, what about Holy Communion? I know one school where the staff and pupil Christian groups got the diocesan bishop to come for their joint communion! Well, why not?

The impact of a Christian group at work or school can be tremendous. Why not give it a go?

42 The Daily Journey

Here's a thought: are you using the time spent travelling to and from work to faith-share? On the train or bus (even the plane), or as you give or get a lift in the car, is it possible to share your faith then? One person in my survey mentioned 'the taxi driver', which I take to mean the regular one: otherwise look at the chapter 'The Complete Stranger'.

There is no set plan with this one, but here are some general principles:

- Be friendly, while not being pushy. Most people are stand-offish, and your kindness will show God's love.
- Be positive about life, including the weather. Most people moan, but we believe that 'this is the day the Lord has made; let us rejoice and be glad in it' (Psalm 118:24), don't we?
- On the bus, train or plane, why not read your Bible or a Christian book? It would soon sort out whether your daily-journey neighbour wanted to talk! A fellow lawyer colleague of mine did that every day, and conversations followed.
- Have Key 4 in mind, praying and watching out for opportunities as the Holy Spirit opens doors.
- National and international disasters and crises often lead to comments, as newspaper headlines shout the problem. My story about the funeral in 'Fellow Workers' may give a clue about wider events. Take the opportunity to speak of your concern, and say that you are praying. Let the conversation take its course.

- These journeys lend themselves to 'one-liners'. As long as you are not corny, a quick comment can be very effective. On my train journeys from London to my home, we pass a church whose whole wall says, 'Prepare to meet your God' (Amos 4:12). A simple quip such as, 'There's a thought – and us doing 80 m.p.h.!' would do.

- If you travel with the same people every day, Key 2 is vital, as you get to know them. You will only have time to know one or two – not the whole railway carriage!

- Don't back off from Christianity, but it's better to talk about Jesus than 'the church'.

- Finally, our 'taxi-driver'. If you are so concerned, then go for it! Talk with him or her. Speak of where you are going, and your spiritual destiny, too. If he belongs to another faith (most in my city do), refer to that earlier chapter. If it feels right, ask him direct questions about whether he knows God: the later chapter on door-knocking has some clues. Taxi drivers are almost always open and chatty, ready for give and take. If the conversation goes on, he won't mind – you are paying! See where it goes.

Use your journeys well. God will bring you alongside those who need you to share your faith with them.

43 Clubbers

Don't get up-tight – this may *not* be your chapter. 'Clubbing' is not for everyone, so if it is beyond you (Key 5) move on! But if you are a 'clubber', read on. The next chapter may help as well.

Basic questions

Before you go clubbing, ask yourself:

- Can I cope with the presence of alcohol and drugs?
- Is God in control of my sex life: opposite and same sex?
- Is God calling me to be a Christian witness in the club? Would Jesus go there?
- Do I understand the club culture? (Check the chapters 'Teenagers' and 'Generation X'.)

If there are problems in any of these areas, don't go clubbing until they are resolved. Your Christian life matters more.

The people

Most clubbers will be at zero when it comes to faith in Jesus or knowledge of the Bible. You may be the very first person to share anything Christian with them. As other chapters have suggested, there will be people of 'peace', who will have a hidden, even subconscious, longing for a real spiritual dimension to their lives. God will lead you to them, as Key 2 helps you get to know people.

If you are not familiar with the club scene, you are in for a shock: it is *very* noisy. Any conversation will need to be in a quiet area and fortunately many clubs do have these. Before you get into verbal faith-sharing, check out if there is a specific group of Christians already doing this – they are about. Clubs in city centres may even have a chaplain. Would your church encourage you and others to undertake this?

Here are two positives which run contrary to much of the rest of this book:

- Key 4 speaks of finding the right time. In the club scene, you may only get one chance, so grab it.
- Key 5 speaks of limitations. Think about this: a number of clubbers may be from Christian homes, where all the efforts of believing family members have failed. Where this is the case, you may be in the right place at the right time to speak in a way no one else can.

Not all clubs gyrate. Some are for older folk or the middle-aged. People sit and chat, and many are lonely. Who from the church ever gets stuck into the Ex-servicemen's or Working men's Clubs? Look back to the chapter on older people. The opportunities here are great for faith-sharing.

The bouncer

One of my favourite answers to the question 'With whom would you like to share your faith?' was 'the bouncer'. And why not? God loves him, whatever his haircut. Basic questions are:

- Does he want to be close enough to you to talk? (Key 5)
- Do you know him well enough? (Key 2)

- Has he got the time? (Key 4)
- Is the doorway the place? (Key 6)
- Where is he at spiritually? You may be starting way, way back. (Key 7)
- Is your church ready for him? (Key 8)

What a lot of tough questions for the tough guy! Jesus specialised in such men, but who's going for them now?

Yes, the club scene is hard. But if God calls you, get lots of prayer support, put on the Ephesians 6 armour, and be there.

44 Pubbers

Do you go to the pub? Very many people do, so why not Christians? You may well not agree, but I think Jesus would go looking for new recruits in our pubs. If you struggle with this idea, rush on to the next chapter. If you feel God's call to share your faith in the pub, you will need to answer the questions at the beginning of the last chapter first, including the ones about drink and sex. The last thing you want is to be breathalysed and found positive!

How to chat

A word of warning: drink talks. After a few drinks people debate for the sake of an argument – which is what you don't want. Be willing to give and take. Your aim is not to prove either that you, or your faith, is right, but to share Jesus in such a way that people are attracted to him. If a 'good' argument is produced, for example, are you strong enough spiritually, and aware enough of your grounds for belief, not to be swayed?

However, the pub is often a good place to share Jesus, because people's guards come down as they relax. You will need to be a good listener. People have problems, objections, wrong ideas, heartaches and even wrongs done to them by the church. Let them talk these through because that is where they are starting from. Your story is also crucial. Your vital relationship with Jesus, and what he is doing in your life, will speak louder than any Bible passage.

As so often elsewhere, Keys 2 and 4 are central: get to

know your fellow pubber and find the right time to talk about Jesus. I talk a lot about football first! If you are going to be a friend, stand your round (if you don't know that means buying drinks when it's your turn, you'd better forget pubbing as a means of faith-sharing!).

Pubbing is a good opportunity for men to share their faith, although of course Christian women have a role too. But the men especially need to think this through: why not get several men in your church to 'adopt the local'? You can encourage (and keep an eye on) each other, and work out strategies for faith-sharing. Furthermore, if you have looked at the chapters on men and the husband, this could be an ideal place to invite outsider men to break the ice of faith-sharing. It is the opposite of Key 5's limitations.

Make conversations natural, letting spiritual things come in and out of chats as other things do. Don't forget the person behind the bar, although you will have to wait until the rush for orders has died down. My experience is that a number of landlords, landladies and bar staff have a keen interest in Christian things and appreciate the chance to talk about them.

Specific occasions

Does your church do anything special for your local pub and its clientele? Never mind asking for their money for the church roof, what about carols at Christmas? If your minister, or a few of you, get on well with the staff, they will welcome a bit of a sing-song a few days before Christmas. You could think about Easter and Harvest, too.

Has your church ever hired the private room in the pub for an event? The landlord would be glad to put on a private bar, and a supper, for a quiz or a speaker. What about a seekers' series, or an Alpha course, or a men-only Bible study weekly?

I know different churches that have done some of these very successfully.

If we are to reach people, we have to go where they are before they come to us. The pub is one of those places. Of course, we want them back at our place, so the church will have to be ready, as will our cell groups, home groups and men's groups. Talk about it as a church, and ask the question, 'Why not?'

By the way, 'lemonade on the rocks' is an OK drink. . .

45 Sports

Sport and Christianity go well together – ask Jonathan Edwards, Bernhard Langer, Va'aiga Tuigamala, Alison Nicholas and Gavin Peacock (if these names mean nothing, this may not be your chapter!). How can you share your faith here?

Watching

What a relief for us older couch-potatoes: we can share our faith while watching our favourite sport! The first secret is to be enthusiastic – about the sport and your faith. It is odd, but you are supposed to be a 'fan' (short for 'fanatic') of a sport, but not 'fanatical' about Jesus. . . .

If you are in a big crowd, the later chapter 'Complete Strangers' applies. Most of us get to know others watching our sport quite well, especially on the coach, car or train travelling to a game. At matches, the one-liner observation – often humorous – may be the best you can do. What about negative remarks? Be gentle! People do swear when excited. I personally struggle with people using 'Jesus Christ!' as an expletive. I follow the advice of a very leading Christian friend when he goes to soccer matches. When someone says those words, his rule is this. The first time, he doesn't hear it. The second, he hears it. The third, he notices it. The fourth, he comments: 'I didn't know you knew my very best friend so well!' It usually works.

Your enthusiasm may enable you to become chaplain to a sports team, especially if you are the minister or a leader at your church. Every team should have a chaplain, whatever the sport. Before making a move, you will get excellent advice from the organisation Christians in Sport (see the 'Helpful Resources' section).

As you watch, and help your team, your faith-sharing should be as much in your style as in your words. See the section on friends for more ideas.

Playing

When involved as a participant, there are great opportunities for faith-sharing, because of the times before and after the game or event when chatting is so natural. Make sure you make time for this, not always rushing away too soon. Here is the man-to-man, woman-to-woman, youth-to-youth opening, with common interests bonding your friendship (Key 2). Naturally, you will not want to talk of spiritual matters all the time (Key 4) – the sport will probably feature more often!

Be a Christian at your sport. My brother Keith always said that Jesus made him a better, fairer, more enthusiastic soccer player. You will need to give time both to the sport and your colleagues: is this where your commitment lies? Get your church to back you in what you do, and help them to see this is a key faith-sharing situation.

As a sports-person, you could be a member of Christians in Sport. They will alert you to other members in your sport, and in your area. There can be wonderful mutual encouragement here. They can give you much better advice than I can on faith-sharing in the sporting area of life. They can also provide good speakers for special events your church could put on. A 'sports evening with . . .' would be hugely popular with many on the edge of spiritual things. Does your church run sports teams? Soccer and cricket work well here, although the question of Sundays is for you to work out.

If you are into sport, then go for this one. You *will* avoid following up 'Well saved!' with the quip 'Did you know Jesus saves?' won't you?! Apart from that, check back to the basic keys, and help your fellow sports fans or players to meet Jesus as you faith-share with them.

46 On Holiday

Holidays can be great times for faith-sharing because people are relaxed and away from normal influences on their lives. Because they are unknown, they can be themselves: the mask of 'this is me at work' or 'this is me with the lads/girls' comes off, and there is a chance to be real, or at least different.

Hello!

Large parts of Key 2 can be truncated: holidays allow 'getting to know you' to happen very quickly, and you find things out as you go along. Here is a golden opportunity to be fun and hospitable – all your best neighbourly styles can shine. It's only for a fortnight! Forgive my nurse-maiding, but please be careful with the male/female friendships.

Before you rush in, do make sure that your holiday acquaintances want you around. We don't want their prejudices about 'dreadful Christians' exacerbated by your heavy style. Do they want to know you? Do they want to talk? Or would they prefer to be left alone? Miserable person that I am, I sometimes prefer the latter!

Sharing

People are more open on holiday. A friend was telling me of a very well-to-do man, sitting with him on a beach at sunset, saying how he wished he had a personal faith. In his business life he would almost certainly not have admitted such a thing. Being relaxed, he was able to open up. Your style should be laid back as well. Talk naturally and happily about your being a Christian: check Key 3 again about your own personal story, which will count for so much. Just be normal – it's not preaching time!

You may well be in the opposite situation to Key 5. The limitations of others do not exist here. As a stranger, there are no close ties to inhibit you. You may be able to walk through spiritual doors which are shut to many others. This is a real time for the Holy Spirit to lead you into good conversations.

One major help may be a local church where you are on holiday. In many centres abroad there are English services. Ones in Africa, for example, may be fantastic. The United States, and some European countries, will have churches in certain places which share Jesus with holidaymakers, with open-air services and barbecues.

More than anything, the ball is in your court. The family in the next caravan or tent, the couple who share your table at the café, the widower alone in the restaurant, the widow on the cruise, may be there in God's purposes for you to share his love with them. As you help them, and share your faith with them, be ready with the advice in Key 7, especially making sure this is not just a holiday thing. Offer to help with Key 8, by finding out about a good church where they live, and getting your minister to contact someone near them, if that would be appreciated.

With all the cautionary warnings in other chapters, the advice here is to be on the look-out for faith-sharing opportunities, and take them in a relaxed way as the Holy Spirit leads. You could be a vital link in someone's spiritual journey.

47 Those in Prison

It was a bit tricky to know where to put this chapter. After all, the person in prison may be a member of your family, a friend, someone from work or a neighbour. I will touch on each as I look at how we can share our faith with someone who is, as they say euphemistically, having a break at the State's expense.

Problems (with answers)

There are one or two obviously unique problems in faith-sharing with someone in prison. Visiting is limited, both with times and length, which means not only fitting in with the authorities but also with everyone else who wants to go, including family. Having said that, my experience is that most prisoners lack visitors, and you can arrange with a parent or spouse not to clash with their time. In closed prisons, especially those rated 'high security', there will be severe restrictions on where you can meet to talk (open prisons are much easier). However, these are challenges to be overcome, and you should not let them put you off.

In a similar vein, do not be deterred by relationship setbacks either. It is almost impossible to imagine what incarceration is like, and your prisoner may well suffer from mood swings and depression. Beware of being conned by them, and be realistic about anything they ask you to do. In particular, be very careful over male/female relationships. Being deprived of a real relationship for a long time will take its toll. I still smile as I recall a visit, 40 years ago, to Strangeways Prison, Manchester. I took a young people's choir to the youth wing for a carol service. A very pretty girl read one of the lessons. At the end of her reading there was riotous applause and whistling from the all-male inmates, with cries of, 'Read us another chapter!' I was glad the warders were present!

You will need to decide how far you are willing to help your prison friend, and how much you will let them rely on you. What will you do on their release, especially if they have no other major outside links? There will be calls for practical help: are you willing to give of your time and money? You will need to set the boundaries.

Opportunities

Despite all these warnings, I want to encourage you to see the very special opportunities you have here. Other members of your family may distance themselves from this 'black sheep'. Neighbours will forget or spurn them. If it is a friend from church, you may be surprised how few care, especially if the offence has been against the church (embezzling the funds, for example). At work, the person will simply become 'history'. You may be the one Christian who will stick with the wrongdoer.

A look back at the chapter on 'drifters' could help. One thing is sure: the person knows they have got it wrong – that's why they are in prison! If there has been a genuine miscarriage of justice (in my experience as a lawyer, this is very rare), you will want to see their solicitor to pursue an appeal. My style would be to encourage the prisoner. Luke 15 is a great chapter: verse 2 has the enemies of Jesus saying that he welcomes 'sinners'. When I preach in prison, or speak to those on probation, I very often talk of the lost sheep, coin or son. Everyone else is telling them how wrong they are and how bad they have been; this message of hope and of God's love brings tears to many eyes.

As you encourage a positive attitude, and help a prisoner meet the Saviour who comes to rescue them, you have a number of plus points to assist you. There is a great deal of time each day for reading, listening to tapes, even possibly looking at videos. A Bible, good books and other resources may be much appreciated. In particular, most prisons have a Christian Fellowship, whose members are there to support the prisoners. Ask at Reception for a contact, or get in touch with the appropriate Prison Fellowship organisation in 'Helpful Resources' at the back of this book.

Every prison has one or more chaplains. They have a particular opportunity to help prisoners. As members of staff, their access is much easier, and they can get alongside your prisoner. They may well value help in the religious services they run, which is another positive for you. With all these helps, getting to faith-share with someone in prison may be a wonderful experience.

There are one or two sorts of people specifically commended by Jesus. Prison visitors are included: 'I was in prison and you came to visit me' (Matthew 25:36). Join the team!

48 The Homeless

When my sister Sue was 21 (we used to celebrate that age, not 18, then!), she told a story at her 'do'. Mum had died nearly six years earlier, and Sue chose one story to epitomise our mother. One day, Sue had come home early from school, to find Mum in the kitchen, washing the feet of a homeless man. She gave him some food and a cup of tea, and off he went. My sister had asked, indignantly, why Mum was doing that for 'that dirty man'. Mum's reply was simple: 'He might have been Jesus.' Sue, and all of us, were deeply moved to recall that incident.

How would *you* cope with a homeless person? Would you want to? Will you act as a Christian, and so share your faith? Ministers' homes especially face this challenge. What can you do?

Be prepared

Decide now what to do if and when a homeless person calls or you meet one in the street. In cities, you could give away all your money and possessions walking down some streets, which is a problem for me in certain African countries. What I do there is carry a quantity of small coins which will buy one meal, and give them away fairly freely. But that is just *my* plan in a specific place. What is yours?

In my own country (England) I would rarely, if ever, give money, for fear of it being spent on alcohol or drugs. I do want to be kind, however. If you help, you will become quickly known. Your home could be a regular stopping place for one or more homeless people. Are you willing for that? Do you know whether the person is wanting food, or money, or other help?

A further question: do you want a homeless person in your home? If you have a young family, or you are entirely alone, you may hesitate (although my mother didn't). If you befriend a homeless young person, for example, where will that lead?

Give real help

I assume that if you are still reading this chapter you want to do something. Here are some ideas:

- You could find out where the homeless person could stay and how they could receive benefits from the State and charities.
- What are any local churches doing? Can the local authority's Social Services Department help? The Salvation Army are a great starting point – and often a finishing point as well, with the fantastic ways they help needy people.
- How does your own church react to needy people? See how your leadership answers.
- Is there a local centre for the homeless? Some churches have special facilities.

All these ways of help are real faith-sharing. If you are going to speak of your faith, you cannot do so without giving practical help: food, clothing and advice on accommodation. It was Bishop Ryle who said, 'If you want to give a tramp a tract, wrap it up in a sandwich.' When you have fed the 'tramp', only then can you talk about Jesus.

But don't back off from the opportunity to say something. If the homeless person has come to your home because you are a Christian, you can show that he or she matters by your care but speak of God's love for them, too.

You may be a very special person to reach out in this way. Jesus spoke with great warmth about people who care for the needy. It is a wonderfully practical way to share your faith.

49 Door-knocking

What scares church members more than anything in evangelism? The idea that they will be asked to go 'knocking on doors'. However, there are those who see this as a wonderful opportunity for faith-sharing. If you are one, this chapter is for you.

Before you start

Are you *sure* this is for you? If you *are* sure, do you go with the blessing of your local church? Even if no one else is going, will your church welcome the positive contacts you make? If not, what will you do with someone who wants to go further spiritually?

Then ask, 'Why am I going?' Churches sometimes pretend they are doing evangelism when they are, at best, publicising their presence and events. If you are into faith-sharing, your aim is to help people come to meet Jesus. Next, do you want to do this on your own, or is it better (and safer) with someone else? Speaking of 'safer', take great care if you go with someone of the opposite sex. I know more than one horror story of a married man and someone else's wife doing 'Christian work' together and ending up leaving their respective partners. Never say, 'It couldn't happen to me.'

You will need a plan before you start. Are you tackling your own road or a street near the church? Would it be a good idea to go through all your church contacts over (say) the last five years – baptisms, weddings, funerals, parents of children and so on – and call on them first? Are you aiming at once a week? Will it be during an evening? How long will you spend?

There is a lot of preliminary planning to be done.

What to say

Before you approach the first door, ask yourself 'Is this convenient?' If the neighbourhood is gripped by a certain TV 'soap', avoid that half hour. When you knock, introduce yourself (a printed card with a photo, signed by your minister, is a good ID), and ask if it is convenient to talk. Feel your way from the start with careful, non-threatening questions.

You must have a plan – variable, but worked out. It is important that you make clear you are from a normal, local church, or the unspoken reaction will be, 'Oh no, the JWs are here.' Say why you have come and, sooner rather than later, say you would like to talk about Jesus.

By this stage you are probably wondering, 'Do I know what I am doing?' The word 'help!' springs to mind. Fear not, excellent help is at hand. A friend of mine, Michael Wooderson, devised a straightforward, user-friendly style of house-visiting for his own church. He has a really excellent booklet about it, which I commend wholeheartedly. Write for details about the booklet *Good News Down the Street* to Grove Books. Further help can be obtained from Evangelism Explosion. (For addresses, see the back of this book.)

Some churches have used the *Jesus* video to great effect, and you could offer this to your contacts. It can be ordered from Agapé. If you plan to leave literature, I have always found the Scripture Gift Mission material to be excellent. Deo Gloria Trust are also very helpful with good literature, as are CPO (the Christian Publicity Organisation).

Are you willing to be a friend, and to take all the time needed, to help a stranger come to know Jesus? It will mean more than one or two visits and a response of 'no thanks' from many houses. But someone is waiting for your visit, and your faith-sharing. Will you go?

50 The Complete Stranger

'I want to share my faith with . . . the Prime Minister . . . a councillor . . . the taxi driver . . . the burglar': all these were responses to our survey. To these we could have added chance encounters on planes, boats and trains or, indeed, anyone we have never met before and are unlikely to get to know apart from that one meeting. What can be done about faith-sharing here?

Speak up

I know a very senior church leader whose style is unique. He gets on a train, opens the door of a first-class carriage, and asks, 'Does anyone here know anything about Jesus?' The great British travelling public averts its eyes. 'Ah – I see you don't. Let me come and tell you,' he goes on, and proceeds to do so with whoever he sits next to. There must be another way. . . .

At least this man gets on with his faith-sharing. Knowing him, he does have a wonderful charm which enables him to get away with it. On journeys, I find many people would like to chat: it soon becomes obvious by their attitude. If so, the conversation is up to you. For example, their early question may be, 'What do you do?' I personally can answer either, 'I'm the director of a charity,' or, 'I'm an evangelist.' Both are true, but the latter gets me into faith-sharing, while the former is a cop-out – though it can of course lead to faith-sharing later in the conversation, when they ask, 'Which charity?'

This is where Keys 1 and 3 combine: knowing what to say, and how to tell your own story, which will count for much. Do you carry any literature? See the previous chapter ('Door-knocking') for possible sources. My friends in the Gideons would have a small New Testament ready to be given away: why not copy them? Your style must be conversational, making space for the other person's questions and comments. It would be embarrassing to ignore Key 2 to such an extent that you gave a 'preach', only to find your companion was a Christian all the time – I have heard of that happening! Conversely, I have heard of people actually becoming Christians through a one-off chat on a plane journey. It could be a God-given opportunity. A direct question may be appropriate at some stage: 'Do you know Jesus?' or, 'Would you like to have a personal relationship with God?' See how it goes: the Holy Spirit is with you in all this.

The taxi driver on a one-off journey would come into the same category here. He won't want a sermon, but may appreciate a chat.

At a distance

Three people were cited to me here, and each is worth a mention.

- *The councillor*: that is, our local elected representative. The constituency member for parliament would be similar. Their lot is to receive negative criticism, so a kindly approach would be welcome. What is your church's attitude here? Do you know your elected representatives at all (Key 2)? Do you, and your local church, pray for them? If your church puts on a special event, they may well respond positively to an invitation to attend. If you feel truly concerned, arrange to meet and share your interest in and concern for them, and take it from there. I enjoy a good friendship with one politician, who often expresses his appreciation.

- *The Prime Minister* and other national and international leaders are a different proposition. I have one international business leader I pray for every day. We have met once briefly. I may be able to do no more, but I remain open to God's leading. I could write and tell him of my prayers – but it must be at the right time. A letter of thanks when a politician does something which helps world peace or the Christian cause is much better than another 'crack' at them.

- *The burglar*. Ah, yes. He's far away. What did he find in your home? Were there traces of Jesus? Perhaps you will help him by forgiving him his trespass against you, and by locking up more carefully to prevent his being led into temptation! We are told to 'pray for those who despitefully use us' (Matthew 5:44 AV). If he is caught, you can meet him at court – or in prison – if you really want to (see 'Those in Prison'). But he must want to as well. Then talk with him, as you would with anyone else.

The general style with complete strangers is first to see whether you can meet them. If you can, and it is a once-in-a-lifetime encounter, then share your story. If you can meet them again, you will have more time to get acquainted (see 'Other Friends'). If you will never meet, prayer and letters are your only resources. But even with a total stranger, there is always something you can do.

And Finally . . .

I was going to do the final dressing-room team talk, getting you all psyched up to get out and do the business of faith-sharing. But I looked again at one of the great Easter readings and changed my mind. There are only two final things to say, from Matthew 28:6–7.

Do you know how wonderful Jesus is, and that he is alive, having beaten sin and death and hell? Remind yourself again:

'Come and see.'

When you are convinced, there is only one possible reaction – to obey the angels:

'Go quickly and tell.'

That's good enough for me! How about you?

Helpful Resources

Please write to me at the following address:

The 40:3 Trust
PO Box 403
Coventry CV3 6SW
Phone/fax 024 7650 4792
Email FORTYTHREETRUST@xalt.co.uk

Other useful addresses:

Agapé
Fairgate House
Kings Road
Tyseley
Birmingham B11 2AA
Phone 0121 765 4404
Email jvp@agape.org.uk

Christians in Sport
PO Box 93
Oxford OX2 7YP
Phone 01865 311 211

Christian Publicity Organisation
Garcia Estate
Canterbury Road
Worthing BN13 1BW
Phone 01903 264 556
Email enquiries@cpo.uk.com

CWR (Crusade for World Revival)
Waverley Abbey House
Waverley Lane
Farnham GU9 8EP
Phone 01252 783761
Email mail@cwr.org.uk

Deo Gloria Trust
Selsdon House
212/220 Addington Road
South Croydon CR2 8LD
Phone 0208 651 6428
Email dgt@deo-gloria.co.uk

Evangelism Explosion
PO Box 552
Southampton SO18 1ZL
Phone 023 8022 8985

Grove Books Ltd
Ridley Hall Road
Cambridge CB3 9HU
Phone 01223 464748

Prison Fellowship England and Wales
PO Box 945
Maldon CM9 4EW
Phone 01621 843232

Prison Fellowship Scotland
101 Ellesmere Street
Glasgow G22 5QS
Phone 0141 332 8870

Scripture Gift Mission
SGM International
3 Eccleston Street
London SW1W 9LZ
Phone 0207 730 2155

Scripture Union
207 Queensway
Bletchley
Milton Keynes MK2 2EB
Phone 01908 856188
Email postmaster@scriptureunion.org.uk

Universities and Colleges Christian Fellowship (UCCF)
38 de Montfort Street
Leicester LE1 7GP
Phone 0116 255 1700
Email email@uccf.org.uk

NB Details correct at the time of going to press, but reference should be made to the *UK Christian Handbook*, published by Christian Research and HarperCollins.

100 Instant Faith-Sharing Talks

by Ian Knox

Essential guidelines on how to talk about your faith, together with 100 outline talks for every occasion, including:

- women's meetings
- youth gatherings
- social evenings
- men's breakfasts
- church meetings
- family services

'A brilliant compilation of practical and biblical help for the evangelist.'

– Stephen Olford

50 Easy Outreach Ideas

by Paul Mogford

You've heard of friendship evangelism – but between earning a living, spending time with the family and church meetings, what time is there for making new friends?

These easy outreach events are designed to be organised with the minimum of fuss for maximum fun and friendship!

From the humble church picnic to a jazz or jive evening, it's all here – all you have to do is open your heart, then open the book.